"As parents, a college education for our children is designed to accomplish many goals. Achieving these goals takes hard work, love, and understanding. *Your Career Fast Track* provides solid personal and career guidance. Based on ten years of working with Roger in the placement of junior executives, and from having gone through the process myself, Roger's perspectives are well thought-out, to the point, and on the mark. I encourage you to consider his message."
— Rand Blazer
Principal, KPMG Peat Marwick

"Roger Cameron knows his business. Listen to him, take his advice, and you will be rewarded with a challenging opportunity in your chosen field. Roger's commitment and dedication helped me make the right career decisions."
— Philip Dobbs
Kraft USA, Inc.

"*Your Career Fast Track* should be required reading for all college-bound high school students, college students, and their parents! Through his years of experience as a professional recruiter, Roger Cameron is intimately acquainted with what it takes to succeed in your career, and can tell it like it is!"
— Raymond H. Smith, M.D.
Diplomate, American Board of Family Practice
FAA Senior Aviation Medical Examiner

"Roger's 26 years of experience was the turning point of my career. I could not have found such a quality job without his teamwork and talent for recruiting. He has his finger on the pulse of the job market. He has my everlasting respect and confidence for matching people to the right job and the right company."
— Elizabeth Franck Volz, Process Engineer
Fiber Optics, Alcatel Telecommunications Cable

"The advice Roger offers you in this book should be required reading for all American youth — particularly for any with the ambition and talent to succeed at the highest levels of Corporate America."
— John P. Dille
Edward D. Jones & Co.

"*Fast Track* is the book librarians have been waiting for. Students who have access to this information will be much better prepared for college and the business world."
— Doris Hill, Librarian
Greenbrier High School

S0-APP-322

"If you want a rewarding, challenging, fast-track career in Corporate America, then this book is your Bible! Roger's fantastic success in placing candidates with great companies looking for future leaders makes him an authority on the skills and background needed to be a success in the job market. This is the book by the insider that you need to start preparing for your career now. Read it, follow his advice, and get the most out of your college career — and life!"

> — Dennis Brooke
> The Prudential Insurance Company of America

"*Your Career Fast Track* offers invaluable information in a concise manner. It is a useful tool for every ambitious high school student."

> — Sue Braden
> North Mesquite High School

"Roger Cameron is the leader in placing young men and women in industry. He knows what is necessary to successfully prepare individuals to meet business needs. He introduced me to industry, and I find what he shared with me then more true now than ever. Listen to him. He will ensure you are prepared to successfully enter the business world"

> — John Jedlicka
> Schneider Specialized Carriers, Inc.

"If you want to know what it takes to get hired by the best corporations in America, Roger Cameron is the one to ask. He has worked with the best of the best and knows what they demand in the entry-level candidate. Don't be caught at graduation without the tools to meet these needs. Follow Roger's advice early in your career preparation!"

> — Allen Koronkowski
> Lever Brothers

"As a college-bound high school student, I am sure you are constantly bombarded with well-meaning advice from parents, teachers, and counselors. While this advice is definitely important, you need sound guidance from an expert — and that expert is Roger Cameron. He has assisted thousands of young men and women in attaining their goals in Corporate America. Roger provided me the opportunity to interview with many of the finest corporations in America, and he can help you prepare for your career also. Read this book now and get a head start on your competition. *Fast Track* is an indispensable handbook to help guide you through college and into your career! Good luck!"

> — Jay Minmier
> Helmerich & Payne International Drilling Co.

"Your Career Fast Track is the most powerful tool in today's market to help you attain career success. Roger Cameron will guide you through every step to ensure that you are headed in the right direction throughout college and into your career. Don't waste a single minute of your time not knowing the precise direction you should be taking. Read this book now, and you will be on your way to attaining your goals. Roger helped me reach mine, and I know he can help you with yours!"

> — Margaret Vallejo
> Johnson & Johnson
> Ethicon, Inc. Division

"Your Career Fast Track is an excellent career resource for high school and college students!"

> — Bob Hazelwood, Counselor
> Naaman Forest High School

"A useful, practical guide which answers the most-asked questions about careers, college preparation, interviews, resumes, and taking responsibility for one's own life plans. Students who have access to this information will be much better prepared for college and the job market."

> — Marjorie Pike, Special Assistant
> Office of Professional Development
> Tennessee Commissioner of Education

"Roger is truly a master of details in the interviewing and job search process — details that can make or break you. *Fast Track* goes beyond the surface, probing into critical areas for long-term success. Roger understands the needs of industry and its ever-changing ways. Reading, absorbing, and then implementing his suggestions will be of the greatest benefit to you. Enjoy and good luck!"

> — Pete Scharfenberg
> Manufacturing Management
> General Mills, Inc.

"Your Career Fast Track is an easy-to-read comprehensive guide on preparing for job success. I recommend it to counselors and students."

> — Ruby Armstrong, Coordinator of Guidance & Counseling
> Garland Independent School District

"Roger Cameron takes the guesswork out of preparing for success in college with his no-nonsense, step-by-step approach. Should be required reading for all college-bound students and their parents."

> — George H. Jenkins, Senior Human Resource Manager
> Mobil Oil Company

YOUR CAREER FAST TRACK
STARTS IN COLLEGE

Develop Your Talents To Win

In A Competitive World

ROGER CAMERON

Odenwald Press
Dallas

Your Career Fast Track Starts In College
Develop Your Talents To Win In A Competitive World

Published by Odenwald Press, Dallas, Texas

Library of Congress Cataloging in Publication Data

Cameron, Roger, 1935-
          Your career fast track starts in college: develop your
          talents to win in a competitive world / Roger Cameron.
1. Vocational guidance. 2. Job hunting. 3. High school students—
Employment. 4. College students—Employment.   I. Title.
HF5381.C2535   1992   650.14—dc20
ISBN 0-9623216-3-X   92-12968
                                             CIP

Printed in the United States of America

Cover design by Ellen Fountain/Fountain Graphics

Acknowledgements

It is appropriate for me to again thank three of our staff for this book, as well as my first book, *PCS To Corporate America* — René Brooks, Mary Lou White, and Leslie Klonoff. They have given me constructive comments over the past many years that have greatly helped me improve my technique and develop as a recruiter. I very simply could not have had so many successes without them.

I would be remiss not to mention the constructive comments and advice given to me over the years by my corporate clients. They have always been fair in their critiques and very gracious in proofing my work. I have always listened closely to their comments and I'm proud that many of these relationships have endured for 26 years.

I am grateful for the many wonderful friends and acquaintances I have from coast to coast and around the world who have encouraged me to write this book. I have listened to their constructive comments, and, also, to their critiques. I thank each of them for making me a better recruiter.

I want to say "thanks" to the hundreds of applicant alumni across America . . . and around the world . . . who are constantly writing me about their great careers and promotions. It makes me feel as if I have had the best job in America these past 26 years. **Each of you makes me proud.**

Once again, to Sylvia Odenwald, my editor and publisher. Sylvia has been adamant that I write this book since the tremendous success of my first book, *PCS To Corporate America.* Sylvia has consistently given me motivation, direction, and, on occasion, a kick to keep the project on schedule. She has a wonderful team, and each of them has significantly contributed to the overall success of *Your Career Fast Track.*

How To Gain The Most From This Book

Your Career Fast Track will be most beneficial to you if you read it early in your college career — or, even better, while you are in high school. Read the book frequently — it may be difficult for you to remember all my points in one reading. Therefore, I recommend that you make a note to yourself to read *Your Career Fast Track* again in 10-12 months. Take out your Day-Timer, Franklin Planner, or whatever method you use for planning, and jot down the reminder now.

As you read the book, use a highlighter pen to mark key points so you can locate them quickly in the future. Stick-on notes are also helpful to use as a method of flagging pages.

Use a tape recorder to practice communication exercises in the book; otherwise, the book will have limited value to you. You need to evaluate your performance frequently so you can improve. Your first attempts may frustrate you, but keep working. The light will break through, and your efforts will be rewarded. You'll be a more confident, aware, and polished person.

I suggest that you not loan this book to others. You will need to use it as a reference and may not have it when you need it. I have calls frequently from people who have to order a second book because someone borrowed the first one and didn't return it. If you think friends or family could benefit from the concepts provided in *Your Career Fast Track*, suggest that they purchase copies or give them as gifts.

CONTENTS

Introduction

In the course of my career as a recruiter for Corporate America, I've gained insights about what is important for young people to consider about their careers. In this book I've given you my discoveries and techniques acquired after years of working with thousands of hopeful applicants.

I've seen many young people disappointed in their career searches. Many have not accepted responsibility for seriously considering their future careers during a very important, formative time in their lives — their high school and college years. They haven't taken advantage of opportunities to develop knowledge and skills that would have helped them prepare to land a first job in the career field of their choice. My message is simple: Take responsibility for your career early in life. Don't accept the idea that as a high school student, you can't initiate the actions necessary to understand yourself, your desires, your strengths, and your weaknesses. One of the definitions of "career" is "the course of a person's life." Your course doesn't begin the day you graduate from college. Every stage in your life is part of this course. Make the most of your experience now. Take it seriously and develop the maturity necessary to improve and grow. It won't always be easy, but the results will be worth it.

I encourage you to take charge of your life **now** before it is too late. Set goals, accomplish your objectives, and learn early in life the pleasure of consistent success. While many people experience occasional success in life, very few achieve the type of consistent success that lifts them into the very top echelon of their age group.

My friend, Walter Hailey, provides the following to consider regarding 25-year-olds' status at age 65: "Out of every 100 people, one will be financially independent, four will be self-sufficient, five will still be trying to make a living, and 90 will be dead broke or dead!" Now that's sad — even pathetic. This situation occurs, not because more people don't have the ability, but because most don't **apply** genetic and developed abilities. Many graduate from college and wonder why their "sheepskin" doesn't enable them to have immediate success. Too many students and non-students fail to realize that knowledge is worthless unless **you** take **action** to apply it. I would hope this book motivates you to a high plane of action. What's most important for you to see and note is the different **degree** of actions that people take. It is well-known that people use only a small percentage of their intellectual ability. Make a promise to yourself right now that you will not allow this to happen to you. Establish quality goals for yourself, educate yourself sufficiently to accomplish them, and then take the necessary action to make it happen. Learn early in life to discipline yourself to do the things necessary for success. Develop yourself in the whole-person concept. Simply stated, this concept maintains you cannot consider yourself totally successful unless you are outstanding in each part of your life.

Therefore, start early in establishing a healthy mind and body. Learn to eat proper foods that will enable you to keep your body at a weight and shape you feel good about. Realize that what you eat severely affects your ability to reason, think clearly, and comprehend. Learn how to dress — which colors and styles enhance your image and which ones don't. Analyze your character strengths and weaknesses, and then determine ways to make correction. Do it now — take action. Analyze your speech, your ability to communicate, your self-confidence, your social grace, and your reading and study habits. Stand in front of the mirror and be honest in self-appraisal. Ask your parents to help in your critiques and to be totally candid and objective. Then, don't get defensive about their feedback, but take action in making corrective adjustments.

Are you aware of the fact that as a college graduate you are in a very elite group? Estimated figures from the National Center of Educational Statistics (U. S. Department of Education) show that 75 percent of young people earn a high school degree. Of those, 45 percent go on to college. And of those who enter college, approximately 23 percent actually receive a baccalaureate degree. As a member of this elite group, you have the responsibility to take your education and do something with it — to take action and develop yourself as a contributing leader. If your neighbor bought a boat and never put it in the water or purchased a car and never drove it, wouldn't you wonder why? I, too, would wonder why anyone would go to college, **hopefully** gain an education, and then do nothing with it.

Going to college does not guarantee an education. That's what this book is all about. Read it, listen to the advice, talk about the advice, and then establish a plan of action for yourself. Put your goals in writing, making sure they are real, attainable, and measurable. Give a copy to your parents and place copies in prominent places, such as on your mirror and refrigerator, and in your backpack. Start now in judging your success relative to your objectives. You'll like yourself better when you have a defined pathway throughout your life.

Be conscious of all the combined forces working against you as you strive to succeed. You'll find others are constantly wanting to divert you from your path to take irrelevant side trips. Realize by their actions, they are saying it's not important for you to walk down your success path. Sadly, too often you listen to them. You become a victim of circumstances. You are always talking to yourself under your breath and kicking yourself for accepting the diversion. But you do have a choice. Determine right now to set your goals and control your environment. On a card write yourself a reminder of your goal: "I will not allow others to divert me from my success path." Good, now you are headed in the right direction.

Some people value a non-profit work experience, while others are more profit-oriented. Once you have completed the career preparation activities suggested in this book, you will have some ideas about the careers in which you are interested. Since my work has been focused in the corporate world, the major thrust of this book is for students who know they want to pursue a career in Corporate America or for those who have not yet made a decision but who are interested in the possibility. However, my recommendations can be helpful to those whose interests lie in the world of non-profit as well.

The book is organized into two major sections. Part I provides ideas for setting and planning career goals, selecting a college, financing school, choosing a major, developing skills independently of academic course work, developing networks, conducting the job search, and preparing your first impression — your resume. Part II supplies a blueprint for interviewing success. **Please** don't make a major error and wait until you graduate to read Section 2. Know **today** what will be asked of you by recruiters. It is much better to know in advance what will be expected. It is more effective to be prepared early rather than have to do your preparation in retrospect. Also, by realizing early what to expect in your interviews, you can potentially alter your "career steps" to be more compatible with employer needs and, therefore, be more marketable at graduation time. In the appendices you will find recommended seminars, books, and tapes for self-development and sample job descriptions to help you examine occupations.

Have fun reading this book. I compliment you for taking the time and effort to read books other than those mandated by your instructors. That action alone puts you at the front of your group. If you will then take my concepts and apply them, you will become an even more outstanding performer. I'll see you at the top of your profession.

Part I: Basic Strategies For College

CHAPTER 1

"Comprehensive and complete. This book is a must read for all
eighth grade students up. The portions devoted to goal setting are
outstanding. I intend to use this as a teaching/counseling aid with
my students."

—Don Bible
Indian Education Specialist
Tulsa, Oklahoma

CHAPTER 1

Begin Early Before College

Planning Your Career

Career choices are so numerous that it can be overwhelming to consider the available opportunities. Think of your career search as a life-long adventure. Realize that a career search is a continuous process. If you are serious about uncovering your potential in life, you will be continually setting goals, questioning yourself about your progress, and growing in new directions. With this self-discovery will come numerous opportunities for career paths.

Sometimes you may struggle with these directions because a lot of the time you will be facing the unknown. Recognize that, due to any number of circumstances, including personal needs, changing career interests, employee layoffs, and business reversals, you may change jobs several times during your life. This is realistic but not particularly desirable. Hopefully, this book will give you insight to make a more accurate career choice early in your life so you can avoid frequent job changes.

I suggest you approach your "what am I going to do when I grow up" search with an action plan that includes the following activities:

- **Explore your interests and aptitudes.**
  One method of uncovering your interests and aptitudes is to take career tests. Career tests may be helpful to you because they provide a general indication of your abilities and interests and possible career opportunities. However, they are only part of the process of developing a career direction. It is important for you to understand this so you don't place too much emphasis on the results.

If you are interested in taking the tests, contact your high school counseling office, college guidance centers, public employment service, or private counseling organizations, and discuss your desire to take the tests. Ask about the organization's services and determine whether they can provide feedback about the results. Also, discuss the cost of taking the tests. Organizations differ in the range of their services. Some may charge hundreds of dollars, others may charge only a moderate fee, and others, such as high school guidance centers, may charge nothing. While there are numerous tests on the market, some of the more popular ones to be aware of are:

- Interest/personality — Myers-Briggs, which measures interests and personality types; Strong-Campbell Interest Inventory, which contrasts interests of successfully employed individuals with those interests you indicate; and, Career Occupational Preference System, which measures job activity preferences or interests.
- Aptitude — Career Ability Placement, which measures aptitudes and abilities based on entry-level job requirements; and Self-Directed Search, which examines aptitudes and interests.

Another method of self-discovery is to spend some quality time recording your interests, aptitudes, and values. High school counselors and career guidance specialists can direct you to career planning guides that provide exercises for inventorying interests, aptitudes, and values. Most people find that writing helps them organize their thoughts and retain information. In the process of gathering information about careers, it will be helpful to you to know yourself well. If you take this step to write down what you know about yourself, your goals and objectives will be clearer, and it will be easier for you to decide what occupations seem like a good match for you as you do your research.

- **Gather career information in an open-minded, systematic way.**

  As you gather career information, be aware of ideas, practices, or concepts that may encourage you to limit your career opportunities. For example, if you are disabled in any way, let go of the idea that you must choose a career that is stereotyped for the disabled. Or, if relatives and family friends have typically selected a certain occupation, which appears to be an interesting and possibly good choice for you, don't close your mind to other possibilities. This time of gathering information is a period of exploration and adventure, of expanding your horizons. You have a lifetime of opportunity before you. Learn now to explore options rather than limit yourself to what you or others already "know" is true or right.

  Organize your information in a way that is effective for you. You may want to use index cards, a notebook, manila folders, a computer, or any other method that helps you organize in an orderly, systematic way.

  Libraries and career guidance centers in high schools and colleges have numerous career research materials for you to investigate. You might start your search at the card catalog or computer index, if the library is computerized, by looking up "occupations," "careers," or "vocations." Don't be timid about asking the reference librarian for help in locating resources or in learning how to use the computer or microfiche equipment.

  Libraries and career centers frequently carry several good occupational reference books. The *Occupational Outlook Handbook*, published by the U.S. Department of Labor, is a reference for occupational information. This resource includes the nature of the work, working conditions, training and educational requirements, advancement opportunities, job

prospects, earnings, related occupations, and sources of additional information. It is organized into 16 broad categories:
- Executive, administrative, and managerial
- Engineers, scientists, and related occupations
- Social science, social service, and related occupations
- Teachers, librarians, and counselors
- Health-related occupations
- Writers, artists, and entertainers
- Technologists and technicians
- Marketing and sales occupations
- Administrative support occupations, including clerical
- Service occupations
- Agricultural and forestry occupations
- Mechanics and repairers
- Construction occupations
- Production occupations
- Transportation and material moving occupations
- Handlers, equipment cleaners, helpers, and laborers

Other good occupational references include the following:
- *Encyclopedia of Careers and Vocational Guidance*, William E. Hopke, editor; J. G. Ferguson Publishing Company.
- *Professional Careers Sourcebook*, Savage and Dorgan, editors; Gale Research, Inc.
- *The American Almanac of Jobs and Salaries*, John W. Wright; Avon Books.
- Bulletins published by U.S. Department of Labor, Bureau of Labor Statistics, such as *Tomorrow's Jobs Overview* (Bulletin 2350-1).

In Appendix E of this book, you will find job descriptions for business and engineering jobs. These descriptions are composites of job summaries provided by numerous individuals I have placed in corporate positions. Use them as an additional source of information about careers that interest you.

A strategy for using these reference books and other materials is to do the following:
- Develop a generic question/answer sheet for your career interests. Make sure it provides sufficient space for you to write each of your answers.
- Set a goal to research one new career a week until you have 15-20 from which to choose.

As you continue your research in the library, you will find that one resource leads to another until you have not only explored the suggested reference books but many other books and periodicals as well. You may also find videotapes or audiotapes that are helpful to you.

Make it a habit to read the business and classified sections of your newspaper. Clip classified ads in the various fields you are exploring. You will begin to find trends in the qualifications that are currently being required for certain positions which could help you determine the curriculum to follow in preparation for a career.

One of your best sources of information may be family and friends. They may be able to answer your career questions or identify individuals you can interview for information. Most people like to help young people and will spend time providing information about their careers. In addition to your personal contacts, be bold about contacting other individuals to set up interviews for career information. Call service organizations such as your local Rotary or Kiwanis Club or Chamber of Commerce officials. Tell them about your interest in exploring careers and ask for referrals to individuals who might be helpful to you.

Be sure to tell those you interview that you are a student and need their help for a career project. Also, make it clear you will take only 10-15 minutes of their time, unless they want to spend more than that. Most businesses are understaffed and people are very busy, so **make sure you do not spend more time than you have stated**. Develop an interview sheet with 10-15 interview questions. Use this sheet during interviews and note the answers you receive. After each interview, send a thank-you note within 24 to 48 hours. Not only is this common courtesy, which you would appreciate if you were extending the favor, but if you continue to be interested in the career, the resource person may be an excellent contact in the future.

Other sources of career assistance sometimes available in libraries and career centers are computer programs that provide career guidance. These systems provide information about a career, such as schools to attend that offer the curriculum for your field of interest and expected salaries. Some software programs consider factors like personal values and lifestyle when supplying information about careers. State governments operate a software program called the Career Information Delivery Systems (CIDS) that provides information about local, state, and national careers. Ask career guidance counselors for information about these systems.

As you consider the information you are gathering about careers, be cautious. In your analysis of potential careers, you may have a tendency to see only the favorable aspects, such as the prestige, money, or glamour associated with them. You may fail to get behind the scenes and do the research to identify those elements that are not compatible with your abilities or skills. I can give a good example of a career choice many students select without appropriate research. I interview hundreds of applicants every year who determined initially that they wanted to be lawyers. They reached their conclusions because of the money, prestige, and glamour associated with being an attorney. After pursuing law as undergraduates, they changed career directions. Very often, they have told me they changed because they couldn't afford law school. After examining their motives further, I have discovered a different reason for their reversals. They changed their direction because they realized that if they wanted to be hired as attorneys by prestigious law firms, they would have to achieve excellent grade point averages from top law schools. They also realized that few would become famous trial attorneys.

I know of **no** career that does not have **both** favorable and adverse factors associated with it. Be sure to examine **all** elements of a profession. Don't lose four of the most important years of your life (college) working toward a very narrow career field. Do your research thoroughly by examining all aspects of your prospective career choices. You might even consider working gratuitously in your prospective career field. This could be done after school or during the summer when you are a student in high school or a freshman or sophomore in college.

If you are a typical American high school student or even a college student, it may not have occurred to you to do your own research. You may have thought this kind of activity was reserved for class assignments only. But think about this research as an adventure in discovery about who you are, what you think, what you like, how you can become the best you can be. Since your future depends upon the effort you make now, isn't it worth spending time developing a strategy for a successful career?

If you find, after your own research, that you would like some additional assistance, you might consider working with a career counselor. In addition to high school counseling offices, counselors can be found in college guidance centers, state employment offices, and community and private organizations. Check the credentials of private counselors with the International Association of Counseling Services (IACS), which accredits counseling services. To receive a listing of accredited services, send a self-addressed, stamped envelope to IACS, 5999 Stevenson Ave., 3rd Floor, Alexandria, VA 22304.

• **Read other career planning guides.**
  There are numerous career planning guides on the market. Here are a few I recommend that I feel are well-written and helpful:
  - *What Color Is Your Parachute?* by Richard Nelson Bolles
  - *The Right Job For You* by J. Michael Farr
  - *Joyce Lain Kennedy's Career Book* by Joyce Lain Kennedy and Dr. Darryl Laramore

• **Study information about occupational trends.**
  The Occupational Outlook Quarterly, printed by the U.S. Department of Labor, Bureau of Labor Statistics, publishes articles that provide valuable information about the employment outlook for the future. According to the Labor Department, "Those graduates who carefully select their career objectives, acquire the most appropriate academic preparation, and are most adept at locating job openings and marketing their abilities will enjoy the smoothest transition from school to work. Others will have to scramble for the best available jobs, risking brief periods of unemployment, relocating to other areas of the country, accepting jobs that do not require their level of education or job-hopping before finding a satisfying position."

Based on current research by the Labor Department, it is expected that increased demand for goods and an expanding economy will result in the creation of millions of jobs in this decade. However, some occupations will have a decrease in employment growth. Knowing which occupations offer the best employment opportunities in the future will be helpful to you in deciding whether you want to enter a field. For example, let's say you are interested in mining engineering. You find that the percent of change in employment between 1988 and 2000 is expected to be only 6%. It is projected that the decreasing demand for coal, metals, and other minerals will result in a slow growth in employment opportunities. You may decide this field is still the most desirable one for you and that you are willing to do what it takes to compete for a limited number of spots. However, you may decide instead to pursue another engineering field, such as electrical engineering, which is expected to have a much faster than average growth.

Since the job market is always changing, you will improve your chances for success by keeping abreast of employment forecasts and analyzing how the changes will affect you.

- **Join clubs and organizations with a career orientation.** There are numerous clubs you can join while you are in high school, such as Junior Achievement, Inc., 4-H Clubs, and Future Business Leaders of America. These organizations provide additional opportunities for you to explore career interests. In college, business fraternities may offer you similar opportunities.

- **Get job experience doing part-time and summer work.** While you are in high school, your most important goal should be to do well academically. Sometimes that is difficult to do if you overload yourself with too many extracurricular activities or take on work responsibilities that are too demanding of your time and energy. You and your family should decide together how you should balance work and school. The benefits of having some work experience during your school years far outweigh the liabilities — as long as you maintain the necessary balance. Consider that students receive numerous benefits in doing part-time work, such as developing communication skills, a sense of responsibility and self-confidence, business contacts, good work habits, computer skills, skill in taking directions, and supervisory skills.

Another benefit of part-time work is that your jobs give you new insights into the world of work you wouldn't have had otherwise. Sometimes this exposure opens up new avenues of discovery that may be very valuable in your career planning efforts.

Making The Most Of High School

In the last several years, many high school students have had an inclination to select risk-free curriculums with lots of electives. With courses like these, they were able to snooze through classes and do more lounging than learning. According to many college officials, the shift today is to more advanced classes. More students seem to be graduating with advanced placement credits.

According to the Educational Testing Service, 1991 graduates who were planning to attend college were opting for more solid academic courses than 1987 graduates. College admissions officials find there is a definite gap in the ability of students who choose basic courses rather than the college preparatory track in high school. They state that even if the students didn't make A's in their advanced high school classes, they do better in college than those who selected easier curriculums and made A's.

My recommendation is that you stretch yourself in high school and choose a curriculum that will challenge you and help you be better prepared for the difficult requirements made of you in college courses.

Establishing Strong Ethics For Your Life

More and more, organizations are stressing the necessity for strong business ethics. Increased dishonesty in various industries has resulted in a rethinking of values. Begin to think seriously about your values and your philosophy of life. High school is a good proving ground for honesty, kindness, patience, fairness, and consideration for others. Now and in the future, standing for right, ethical behavior will not always be easy. No matter what difficulties you incur, your reputation and your "course in life" can only be strengthened by strong ethics and behavior.

Setting And Achieving Career Goals

You now have some very definite suggestions about how to go about your career preparation. Only you can make it happen. To do this, you'll actually be practicing and improving skills that prove to be very desirable in a candidate for professional positions in Corporate America — planning, time management, persistence, initiative, and self-confidence.

The first step is to establish your plan. What are your goals? When can you reasonably achieve them? What will be your interim goals in achieving your long-term goals?

Let's say you are now a sophomore in high school. Perhaps a three-year plan is in order. Your long-term goals are to identify a strong career interest, to select a college and a major, and to determine how you will finance your college expenses — all to be accomplished by the middle of your senior year. Think about each of the activities we have recommended for planning your career, read further in this chapter about some ideas for selecting a college and planning financial aid, and then develop your plan. Set up a schedule of weekly and monthly actions you will take. Identify specific times you will accomplish activities, such as going to the library, joining a club, participating in organizational activities, and mailing letters for scholarship information. Make sure you check off your accomplishments. Do a quarterly review of your progress to see if your plan is working and if you can reasonably expect to accomplish your goals with the plan you have developed. Adjust your plan as necessary to help you accomplish your goals.

Choosing Mentors

Choose two mentors — if possible, before you enter college. However, if you are already in college, it's still not too late to secure mentors. The reason for selecting **two** mentors is because everyone has some biased opinion. It is good to have a balance of opinions to measure one suggestion against another. While both viewpoints may be accurate, combining the two opinions will give you confidence about the information you are receiving. I would recommend that you talk to your parents and their friends and contacts to identify people who have been successful in the corporate world. At least one of the mentors should work for a top Fortune 500 company. While it may not be your ultimate career choice to work for a Fortune 500 company, I assure you that any guidance you receive will give you many options for career opportunities.

Choose people to be your mentors who can give you accurate insight and quality information in a timely manner. I cannot imagine any successful corporate person who wouldn't be honored to give guidance to a young student. Any successful corporate manager has had to interview many young men and women, as I have, and has had to rule them out for what they did not accomplish in high school and college. Why wait until you are out of college to find out what you should know **before** college?

New college graduates often have a significant degree of naivete about business. Recruiters today are more and more adamant about hiring people with good "street savvy" or business sense. Some "real world" professors can help you attain this knowledge but not as consistently as good business mentors. Make a conscious effort to graduate from college with a good business sense.

The kind of mentors you want are extremely busy people. They are successful individuals. They are professionals with major corporations who make significant contributions to their companies

— who accomplish difficult business objectives. Often, it is better for you to write them letters regarding questions you may have, or when you do call them, give them an option of two or three possible times they can speak with you. More than anything else, when you have received information, take the time to write a thank-you letter within 24 to 48 hours. Following your graduation your mentors may be able to refer you to people within their own companies or other companies who may have an interest in hiring you.

Let your mentors know what your strengths have been, what you like to do, and the extracurricular activities in which you participated during your high school years. Give them some insight as to what it is you want to accomplish in your life. Let them know what things excite you in a career. It is also helpful to be very candid about your financial status. Any advice given to you must be compatible with your personal financial situation. Prepare a resume and give copies to your mentors. The more information you can give them about yourself, the more accurate their insight and advice can be. I encourage you not to miss this critical activity of having mentors as you head off to college.

It is also valid for you to have mentors as you start your career in Corporate America. They can be extremely important to you in choosing the right career paths. Don't try to make all of the decisions on your own. Look back over your lifetime and you will see that not every decision you made was a good decision, even though you may have thought so at that point. Since a mentor may be able to help you make better decisions in the future, I would encourage you to take advantage of that relationship.

Selecting A College
You must be very careful in selecting a college that is right for you. Many of my client companies suggest that it is better to choose a college where you can be assured of obtaining a high grade point

average versus going to a better school where you graduate in the middle of the class or even lower than that.

You need to examine yourself very thoroughly. Be honest with yourself. Measure yourself by others with whom you have competed in grade school, junior high, and high school. Do not mislead yourself. Many of the most successful people in the world have average academic skills but have succeeded because of their attitudes to apply their God-given abilities. We can't all go to Harvard, Stanford, or Wharton, but we can all choose a college where we can produce the kind of grade point average it will take to be hired in Corporate America. I'm not suggesting that you select an easy school. I am suggesting that you measure your ability very carefully and choose a school where you will not only stretch your capabilities but also excel. **Your goal should be to graduate with a 3.5 GPA or above.**

It isn't important where the college is in location to your home. It isn't important to go to the college where your friends go. Selecting a college is a very individual decision and should again be made on the basis of what is best for you. Both large schools with big enrollments and smaller schools have advantages. For example, larger schools may offer better curriculums for your field of study while smaller schools may provide smaller classes with more individual attention.

Students have many reasons for low grades: "I went to a tough school." "Grades were easy for me in high school, but when I went to college, I fell behind." "My grades were low because I worked my entire way through college." These "reasons" are **excuses** for poor planning. If you use them when you interview for a job, you may be viewed as an individual who uses poor judgment, who doesn't know how to plan well, or who doesn't apply himself or herself to a challenge. If you have carefully selected the right college for you, if you have planned college financing without having to work and go to school simultaneously as I suggest later, and if you apply yourself to your academic studies with persistence and enthusiasm, you will have a good chance of getting excellent grades.

There is a wonderful world waiting for you if you take the time to organize your career objectives, prioritize those objectives, and then accomplish what you have set out to do. It's like being a "top gun" fighter pilot. You must think way out in front or you lose. Once you are behind, it's almost impossible to catch up.

Using College Catalogs And Guidebooks

Now for some practical ways of getting started in your search for the right school. College catalogs and guidebooks that can be used as resources for selecting a college are numerous. You can find these reference materials in libraries and school counseling offices. Some of these resources list individual schools, others list colleges in a state or region, and others list all four-year colleges and universities in the country.

Additionally, computer software programs are available that speed a student's search for a school. Peterson's and The College Board are two of several publishers of college and financial aid guides which offer this kind of software program. These programs enable students to identify schools that meet their specific requirements, such as geographical area, major, and housing needs. With this software, students can quickly print out a list of the schools meeting their criteria. Check with your school or local library to determine if these programs are available.

While computer programs provide a streamlined method of locating suitable schools, they do not provide in-depth information about the schools. For more extensive data, students can use the guidebooks.

> **Remember:**
> **College = Education**
> **Education = Comprehension**
> **High Comprehension = High Grade**
> **Point Average**

Financing College

There are many ways to finance your college education. First of all, your parents can pay your way through college. They can do it as a gift or they can loan you the money. I have applicants tell me, "I didn't want my parents to pay my way through college, so I worked. That's the reason I have a low grade point average." If working your way through college will lower your GPA, then borrowing the money from your parents and getting a high grade point average is a good strategy. After graduation you can get a job earning more dollars than you could earn in part-time work during college, and then you can pay your parents back. Don't forget to pay your parents a fair interest. They will be eager to help a **responsible** son or daughter.

If your parents can't help you, how about a relative — an uncle, aunt, grandmother, or grandfather? Determine when you will pay the relative back and put it in writing to remind you of the importance of this responsibility and of your appreciation for the one who helped you get that wonderful education. To borrow family money and not pay it back is the same as borrowing money from a bank and not repaying it.

Be creative in determining where and how to get financial support. For example, you could consider requesting a loan from a private investor. (You can find names of investors in the want ad sections of newspapers.) You could suggest that the loan be based on interest return or a percentage of your gross earnings for 1-10 years. In the latter case, you would need to do some research to estimate your potential earnings during this period so you could present a fair investment. Because a loan of this type could be termed a higher risk loan, you must offer high-risk return. For example, you might also want to offer the investor a life insurance policy equal to the loan. If an individual finances your college education — for example, for law or medical school — I believe you would quickly see the merit in this form of financing. Remember, be innovative. Your education is worth it.

I encourage you to decide how you are going to finance your entire four years of college **before** you go. Determine how you're going to finance college in a manner that allows you to concentrate on your education, not how you are going to scrape by. Don't go to college thinking that everything will work out. That's really not the reality of life. Take the time to sit down and ask yourself, "Are my parents going to pay for my college? Am I going to have to earn my way through college? How can I secure loans? Can I get scholarships? Should I take ROTC and attempt to have the military pay for my education by owing them several years after graduation?" Begin early to think about this. Ask your counselor at school or personnel in a local city or university library if they have computer software that will enable you to search for financial aid opportunities at the schools you have targeted. As I mentioned earlier, Peterson's and The College Board, as well as other publishers, have developed financial aid software that makes this search easy and fast. You enter family financial information, the colleges you have selected, academic information, and interests. By estimating your family's expected contribution, which is based on federally approved formulas, the programs can provide a financial aid profile of the listed colleges. Also available through most programs is a list of scholarships for which you may be qualified.

Be sure that your career objectives and your ability to finance your education are compatible. I've interviewed many individuals who chose to study for a law or medical degree. However, students with these career objectives frequently are not realistic about the financial commitment required for these career choices. Often, their funds become exhausted, and they feel they cannot afford further schooling. They are left with undergraduate degrees in liberal arts, biology, or chemistry, which are not always considered relevant degrees in business. Don't let these situations happen to you. Wake up now to the real world. Be certain you have the financial ability to fund your career choice. If you are at all interested in a career in Corporate America, don't get an undergraduate degree with a curriculum that is not valued in the job market. It could mean that you have to get an advanced degree to qualify for a position. Most parents I know plan for their children's undergraduate degrees and are fortunate if they can afford that much education.

Obtaining Scholarships

When you think about the fact that there are tens of thousands of scholarship and grant sources and that much of the scholarship assistance is never awarded, it seems worthwhile for you to spend some time researching scholarship opportunities. There are many publications that can tell you how to obtain scholarships offered by schools or private companies and foundations.

Most school or public libraries have copies of three reference books that list scholarships. *The College Blue Book* (Macmillan Press, 866 Third Avenue, New York, New York 10022) lists scholarships, grants, and loans. *Peterson's Annual Guide/Undergraduate Study* (Peterson's Guides, Princeton, New Jersey) is a guide to two-year colleges and lists scholarships available in these institutions, and *Barron's Profiles of American Colleges* (Barron's Editorial Services, Inc., 250 Wireless Blvd., Hauppauge, NY 11788) provides descriptions of four-year college scholarships. About 80 percent of all scholarships available are awarded by the colleges themselves. Additionally, The American Legion publishes a financial aid guide which is a bargain for $2. The title is, *Need a Lift? Educational Opportunities, Careers, Loans, Scholarships, Employment, An American Legion Service for Young People.* (Send your check to The American Legion, National Emblem Sales, Box 1050, Indianapolis, Indiana 46206.) The guide also contains a coupon for a quality personalized electronic scholarship search at a reduced price of $15. A reference guide that is helpful because it categorizes financial aid by career field is *The Scholarship Book, 3rd ed.,* by Daniel J. Cassidy and Michael J. Alves (Prentice Hall trade paper, 1990, $19.95 in bookstores). Another very helpful reference that provides a lot of information for price-sensitive students is *The College Price Book 1990: How to Find an Affordable College,* edited by Dr. John Minter and Thomas E. Giska (Higher Education Publications, 703-532-2300, $23 by mail).

You should apply for these scholarships no later than early September of your senior year in high school by contacting the financial aid office at the college or colleges you have selected. As a matter of fact, many scholarships go unused every year because no one applies for them. Be creative in looking for scholarships. Interestingly, the better grade point average you achieve in high school, the more scholarships you can receive. Be conscious of that. Remember, too, that although you may not receive a scholarship your freshman year in college, scholarships are available for the other three years. If you can finance your first year and do well academically, you may have an even better chance at scholarships your three remaining years.

Angel Ragin is a graduate of Northeast Comprehensive High School in Macon, Georgia. Angel began thinking about how she would finance her college education when she was in the seventh grade. On September 15, 1991, she was featured in an article in

Parade Magazine - "How to Get to College—On Your Own." Angel is bright, was third in her class, and had combined SAT scores of 1190. As president of the student council, editor of the literary magazine, and president of the science club, she was also a leader in her high school. She was able to maintain her grades, participate in extracurricular activities, and still work 30 hours a week. But what is most interesting about Angel is her determination to finance her education. As a result of her research and work, she was offered more than $315,000 in college scholarships.

Angel began her pursuit during the summer before her senior year by reading brochures about scholarship programs. She then made application to seven colleges, and six of these offered her scholarships. She also applied to foundations, institutions, and companies and received additional scholarships. Angel offers encouragement to other students who have to be creative in financing their education. *Parade* quotes her as saying, "Anybody who has talent should be able to do what I did. It can be done." She also offers this advice to other students who may be depending on their parents for guidance: "Numerous people have written me, asking for help for their daughters and sons. I don't mean to be rude, but it's the daughters and sons who should be writing. What it says to me, if your parents are writing, is that **you** don't have the motivation." Angel has said it so well. The opportunities are there for you. The most common excuse I've heard for not applying is that "there are so many applications, I get tired of them." Completing applications for financial aid is **not** as hard as working your way through school. **It's up to you** to be creative, to work hard, and to go get them.

Securing Loans

If parents or relatives cannot provide funds for college and you are not able to qualify for enough scholarship money, think seriously about securing loans. It is very common for college students to apply for loans. In fact, according to the Student Loan Marketing

Association (called Sallie Mae), about 60 percent of college students received monetary aid of some type (scholarships or loans) in 1990. A variety of loans are available to students, some of which are sponsored by the federal government. To get advice about applying for these loans, contact college financial aid offices. For information about commercial loans and some federal programs, contact your local banks.

The regulations for repaying loans are not all the same. Some loans must be repaid while you are a student, while others allow a 6-12 month grace period after graduation before payment is begun. Some loans are made to students who then are legally responsible for repayment of the loans, while others are granted to the parents who then are responsible.

The following are loans and grants sponsored by the federal government:

- Pell Grant — This is the largest federal grant program. An undergraduate who receives a Pell Grant may receive up to $2,300 per year.
- Stafford Loan — This is a federally sponsored loan and the most frequently granted of this type loan. In the past it was called the Guaranteed Student Loan. Freshmen and sophomores can receive up to $2,625 each year, juniors and seniors up to $4,000, and graduate students up to $7,500.
- Perkins Loan — This is a federally sponsored loan, previously called the National Student Defense Loans. The loan is available to undergraduate and graduate students, is based on need, and has a 5 percent interest rate.
- HEAL Loan — This is a federally sponsored loan available to students who want to enter health professions. Loans range from $12,500 to $20,000 annually, depending on the field of study.

- PLUS Loan — This loan is federally sponsored for parents, is available without regard to need, and can supply from $4,000 a year to a maximum of $20,000.

Working Through College

We have recommended that you not take college courses and work at the same time unless you are confident you can maintain high grades (3.5 or higher) while working. One strategy could be to alternate work and study semesters — working for a semester and then going to school for two semesters. Remember that it is more important to take time off to earn money so when you are in school, you can give 100 percent of your time to concentrate on your studies to secure a high comprehension level.

Cooperative Education Programs

If you have no objection to alternating work and study periods, consider cooperative (co-op) education programs that allow you to earn money to finance your college tuition and living expenses. During the periods that you work, you are paid a salary by the participating company. The salary you command is influenced by your college major, the level of responsibility you assume, and the quality of work you do. On a national average, a college student can earn $7,500 a year in a co-op program.

Co-op programs for undergraduate and graduate students can be found at approximately 1,000 colleges and universities in the U.S. These programs are available in two- and four-year college programs and, to a limited degree, in five-year programs. Community colleges generally offer parallel programs, with the student spending part of the day in class and part on the work assignment.

Opportunities for work can be found in a wide spectrum of career situations. According to the National Commission for Cooperative Education, an estimated 50,000 employers hire co-op students. The largest employer of co-op students is the federal government, which employs 16,000 students through 36 federal departments. Additionally, co-op jobs can be found in national or international firms, local or regional companies, or public interest organizations. Depending on the policies of the school you attend, you can obtain your co-op assignment with the same employer, concentrate in the same field but with different employers, or change fields with new employers.

Most programs charge tuition rates for the co-op program because the schools give academic credit for the work experience. However, other programs grant no academic credit and, therefore, charge no tuition. Some programs levy a separate cooperative education fee.

The advantages of participation in a co-op program are numerous. Consider that participation in a co-op program provides the opportunity for you to:

- Gain professional work experience.
- Integrate your college curriculum with actual professional experience in your field.
- Have short-term opportunities to test a variety of career fields.
- Have an opportunity to work your way up in an organization before you graduate from college.
- Work with a co-op coordinator with knowledge of companies and connections in your field of study.
- Establish professional connections of your own.
- Earn as much as $7,500 per year during participation in the program, allowing you to help pay your college tuition and expenses.
- Receive job offers as you approach graduation. (According to statistics, 80 percent of co-op students receive offers for full-time employment from one of their co-op employers.)

• Command a higher starting salary, move up the career ladder more rapidly, and receive merit raises and promotions more frequently than those not participating in co-op programs.

There are many good reasons to consider the co-op plan. If the opportunities appeal to you, your next step will be to determine which colleges and universities offer co-op programs. The *Cooperative Education Undergraduate Program Directory* lists these schools, their locations, and their programs and provides a few of the national and international employers who hire co-op students regularly. You can order the listing from the National Commission for Cooperative Education, 360 Huntington Avenue, P. O. Box 999, Boston, MA 02115.

Obtaining Military Scholarships

Another way to finance your college education is through a military scholarship. Many colleges and universities enable students to participate in military training programs on campus. These programs provide an opportunity to qualify for commissions in the armed services while attending college. The programs for the Army and Air Force are the Reserve Officers' Training Corps (ROTC) Programs and for the Navy and Marine Corps, the Naval Reserve Officers' Training Corps (NROTC) Program. Many schools that do not have the programs on campus have established agreements (called cross town agreements) with schools in close proximity so that students can still participate in an ROTC program.

Depending on the program, one-year to four-year scholarships are available. If you are considering a military scholarship, be sure you understand exactly what the benefits and responsibilities are. In order to apply for and maintain a scholarship in these programs, a student must meet general eligibility requirements and specific academic, physical, and legal requirements. Depending on the program and the number of years of scholarship for which you apply, the requirements differ. For example, some of the qualifications common to the programs include the following:

- Be a citizen of the U.S. and at least 17 years old before the scholarship becomes effective.
- Apply for and gain admission to an ROTC or NROTC college or colleges.
- Achieve qualifying college entrance examination scores. [Winners of NROTC scholarships typically have Scholastic Aptitude Test (SAT) or American College Test (ACT) scores that fall in the top 10 percent nationally. Sixty-seven percent of those selected for Army ROTC four-year scholarships for the 1988-1989 school year had SAT scores in the 1200-1600 range or ACT scores from 27 to 36.]
- Be a high school graduate or have equivalent credit and have good grades.
- Pursue an academic discipline approved by the ROTC or NROTC program you are entering.
- Meet required physical standards.
- Be accepted by a college that hosts the ROTC or NROTC program to which you are applying.
- Participate in leadership, extracurricular, and athletic activities (or for students who hold part-time jobs and do not have enough time to participate in these activities, receive credit based on the number of hours worked per week).

High school students who are interested in a four-year scholarship should apply in the last half of their junior year or by December 1 in their senior year. Selection of winners is based on the results of an interview; a physical examination; the SAT or ACT test results; high school academic standing; and extracurricular, leadership, and athletic activities.

The financial benefits of ROTC and NROTC scholarships are significant. Uniforms are provided; most tuition and on-campus educational expenses are paid; and a flat rate for textbooks, classroom supplies, and equipment is provided. Additionally, you receive an allowance up to $1,000 each school year the scholarship is in effect. You are also paid when you attend summer training camp.

In return for the assistance you receive in obtaining your baccalaureate degree, you are required to accept a commission and serve in the active or reserve military for eight years. In the Army you may fulfill this obligation by serving two to four years in active duty followed by service as a citizen soldier in the Army National Guard (ARNG) or U.S. Army Reserve (USAR), or you may serve a period of active duty necessary to complete an officer basic course followed by eight years of service in the ARNG or USAR. Air Force ROTC and Navy-Marine Corps NROTC scholarship graduates who are commissioned must serve a minimum of four years active duty.

To get more information about the Army and Air Force ROTC and Navy-Marine Corps NROTC programs, talk to your high school counselor or contact the ROTC or NROTC office at the college or university of your choice.

The ROTC program can have tremendous benefits for the right person. However, I want to caution you about going into ROTC. Over the years I have interviewed thousands of military officers and heard stories such as, "My ROTC instructors told me that education wasn't really where I should put my emphasis. They urged me to put more energy into leadership roles in ROTC because that would serve me best as I entered the military as a commissioned second lieutenant, a lieutenant, or an ensign entering the Navy." The point is that over 70 percent of all ROTC graduates leave the military prior to retirement. They exit the military generally in a five-year, six-year, or seven-year period of time. Then, they knock on the door of Corporate America and want industry to hire them. Industry evaluates the college education, looking first at the relevancy of the curriculum itself and then, secondly, at the comprehension rate

(GPA). So, never let anybody convince you for any reason that there is anything on a college campus more important than the education itself.

> ### #1 Objective in Going to College
> ### College = Education
> ### Education = Comprehension
> ### High Comprehension = High Grade
> ### Point Average

As we've said, if you want to be involved in an ROTC program, it is very important to evaluate your ability to concentrate on your studies and get the grade point average you want while you are involved. ROTC has many functions you are required to attend. With proper allocation of time and prioritizing, you can do both ROTC and your academics. I have seen it done in thousands of cases. Many individuals who were in the ROTC program actually tell me that because they knew they had a job when they graduated, they felt it unnecessary to be concerned about grades or, for that matter, the curriculum. They didn't realize that one day they might want to leave the military and interview with Corporate America, but if they had done proper research, they would have discovered the high odds of that happening.

If you enter the military, you should expect to be one of those individuals who leaves the military prior to retirement. After all, if over 70 percent of the people leave, it is highly possible you will be one of them. Therefore, you will want to recognize the importance of education if you want to obtain a good position in Corporate America.

Choosing A Military Career

Yet another factor you should consider in your ROTC experience is your choice of specialty within your branch. Some specialties provide experience that will be more valuable to you in establishing a career in Corporate America than will others. A common denominator of the most marketable specialties is **leadership**.

Look at it from Corporate America's perspective. Let's say you choose not to enter the world of profitability immediately upon graduation. When you do so four to seven years later, Corporate America will determine whether your experience in the military has equaled or exceeded what you could have had in a corporate position during that same time. While your initial experience in Corporate America is challenging and rewarding, it rarely matches the **leadership** training and **practice** that the military can give you.

So, while military intelligence may sound intriguing, it is not a strongly marketable specialty because it does not provide leadership training that is as extensive as the "combat arms" specialties. Consequently, companies are much more likely to take the combat arms officer (in the Army — infantry, armor, field artillery, engineer, air defense; in the Navy — nuclear power, surface warfare) instead of the military intelligence officer.

If you are going to leave the military and go into the FBI or the civil service, then military intelligence can be a very good field for you. However, that means you intend to spend your career in the world of nonprofit. Be very careful about that. There is nothing wrong with it if it's right for you, but there is a significant difference between the operating philosophy of the nonprofit world and the world of profitability. I have recruited **capitalists** for over 25 years and have a very strong belief that performing in the world of profitability is one of the most fulfilling and rewarding careers a person can have. To ensure your future marketability in the event you desire to leave the military prior to retirement, predetermine the military career that provides the most relevant skills and experience for Corporate America.

Corporate America values the skills and experiences that military officers bring with them after their first tour of duty at ages 26-30. Most officers have high morals, a strong work ethic, self-motivation, poise, maturity, and an ability to make things happen. They are also creative, resourceful, excellent "team" players and extremely goal-oriented. They have been conditioned to fight through adversity to accomplish their missions.

Many officers develop valuable knowledge and skills in areas such as engineering, logistics, finance, data processing, and human resource development. The Air Force and Navy consistently develop very experienced engineers. These branches are more technical in nature and have more engineering positions available. However, outstanding engineers are recruited from all branches.

Joining The Air Force

Remember that there are some great positions in the Air Force other than pilot or navigator. As a matter of fact, these two positions are **really not at the top of Corporate America's list**. While pilots and navigators have tremendous responsibility and are usually outstanding individuals, they do not develop supervisory skills comparable to many line officers, particularly in the area of maintenance where the officer in charge has supervised from 150 to 200 people.

Also, in the Air Force there are excellent engineering programs at Hanscom Air Force Base in Boston, Massachusetts; Wright-Patterson Air Force Base in Dayton, Ohio; and Los Angeles Air Station in Southern California. These bases are primarily research-oriented. We're able to get some of the best engineers the military has to offer from these bases. Some of you who have chosen engineering and want to get into a research environment might like to go in this direction. You would develop some very strong skills to help you transition into Corporate America should you make that decision.

Joining The Navy

One of the best military programs is the Navy nuclear power program. This program is a good choice for the college graduate in the Navy NROTC program with a high GPA in engineering. This is not to suggest Corporate America doesn't also find outstanding individuals from surface warfare, supply, general administration and other career fields. As a matter of fact, we have more companies who seek out the Navy nuclear power officer over any other person in the military. Another very fine Navy program is the surface warfare program. Most officers from these programs have held strong leadership roles. These programs are highly recommended to those of you who enroll in the Navy NROTC programs.

Choosing Your Curriculum

After selecting a college, you must choose the curriculum that fits your aptitude and ability. Basically, there are two ways to achieve a top position in Corporate America — through business or engineering. For students intent on a corporate career, graduating from college with a technical degree would be an advantage because the majority of Fortune 500 companies are becoming more "high tech" in nature every day. Whether companies are in a manufacturing or service business, they want and need to hire the quantitative, analytical mind. This is not a realistic direction for every student because not all have the necessary high math comprehension, nor is it what every student wants to do. **It's just a fact that most college graduates with an engineering degree are paid a higher salary as they enter Corporate America. Those with high grade point averages are paid even more.**

If you choose engineering, consider the engineering degree that will offer you the broadest career choices — mechanical engineering. The mechanical engineer can enter almost any industry within the Fortune 500 industries, such as aerospace, paper, chemical, and electronics. This is not to suggest that mechanical engineering is more important than others. All engineering curriculums have equal importance. However, some have less market versatility than others. We have occasionally witnessed a poor market for electrical engineering or chemical engineering majors depending on certain economic conditions. **As well, no matter which engineering degree you choose, it will be more valuable today if you have a heavy computer emphasis.** Corporate America is no longer looking for the average ME, EE, or IE. Virtually every technical function today is computer-aided.

If you choose a business degree, you also have many options — finance, accounting, business administration, marketing, data processing, management information systems. All of these are excellent degrees that allow you career flexibility when you interview at the placement office. Again, these degrees must be supplemented with a heavy knowledge of computers. There is virtually no process in America today that is not computer-based, no matter what the field.

Ideally, when you go to college you should have two computers and a printer. One of the computers should be for your room and the other should be a laptop you can use at the library or in the classroom. Make one of your objectives to graduate with strong computer literacy. Two years ago, I could recruit people for Corporate America whom I wouldn't even think about recruiting today. To remain competitive in the interviewing world, the graduate must have a degree that is computer-based, whether it's in a business program or an engineering program.

If you choose a career other than in engineering or business, that is fine. However, I would like to point out a problem that comes to my attention many times. Students often choose careers, such as park ranger, lab technician, counselor, or teacher. These careers are good choices for many people; however, students can expect lower compensation with these positions than with engineering or business positions. Often, students wait until they graduate to decide they are more capitalistic than they thought and would like to have more money — perhaps, even a lot more money than these positions will offer them. Be certain you have done the research I have suggested and know what is important to you. While it's impossible to examine your whole life in advance, it is necessary to ask yourself many questions about what kind of lifestyle you value and how you want to live in the future.

Selecting A Major

Unfortunately, many college students choose a major for the wrong reason—because they enjoy it. Maybe that's okay if the curriculum enhances their career. If not, after four years of enjoyment, then what do they do? I firmly believe the purpose of college is to lay an academic base for building a career. Unless someone is going to support you and give you whatever you need, you should select an academic major that ensures a successful career.

Do yourself a favor. Do your research before you make such a major decision. Spend time investigating your chosen field. Look at both the positive and negative aspects. You must accept a career field for what it is.

Gaining Maturity

Students often excuse a low GPA. They may say, "I matured later in life. When I went to college, I wasn't really ready for college or to be on my own. It wasn't until my junior year that I finally realized the importance of education, but by that time it was too late. I had a low GPA. While I did very well the last two years of college, I wasn't able to bring my grade point average above a 2.5." Don't start college knowing you are immature. Do something about it. Confide in your parents and say, "Look, I want to spend my summer before college going to a motivational program. I want to get to know myself better and learn how to deal with my weaknesses and strengths. I want to learn better how to prioritize, organize, and effectively manage my time. I want to learn how to set difficult objectives, break them down into components, and accomplish them. Will you help me?" There are few parents who wouldn't help their child to better prepare for success in college, but their child has to talk to them. If you want this help, discuss your goals and concerns with your parents. In addition, you have to talk to yourself. An immature high school student is much like anyone else. Unless a person is willing to be candid and admit to himself that he needs help, he can't help himself, and no one else can help him.

If you have a sense of insecurity or immaturity, there's nothing wrong with that. Many students experience this as they graduate from high school and transition into college. As a matter of fact, many of us didn't have our priorities straight when we went to college. We wanted to get away from home and our parents and be able to run our own lives. We sat through the entire summer before college deciding exactly how we were going to fail. Instead of planning for failure, why don't you plan for success? The first thing you have to do is be honest with yourself and your family. Then, you have to do something about it. Control your life. Don't let your life be controlled by a set of circumstances.

As I look at applicants' interests and hobbies, I smile when I find a young person who is reading motivational books. Few do. When I interview an individual who does, I am somewhat biased. Even before I start interviewing, the applicant is a step up in the interviewing process. I couldn't begin to count all of the motivational books I have read. I can honestly tell you I have never read one that didn't teach me something new or that didn't remind me of things I could be doing better.

Applicants often say, "Oh, I know all that stuff." **Knowing it** is irrelevant. The question is, "**Do you use it?** Do you really believe you can be what you want to be? Do you really believe you have the power within yourself to become a tremendous success — not only in college but in your chosen career path? Do you really believe you can achieve those private goals you have in your hip pocket?" I'm here to tell you that you **can** — if you really believe.

Individuals have said to me, "Well, I don't believe in motivational books. I am what I am." That's an interesting statement, isn't it? "I am what I am." What these people are saying is they can't improve. This is not true. You **can** improve yourself. You can grow.

Rarely do I see anyone willing to spend money to improve themselves. I venture to say only one student in a thousand actually reaches in his back pocket, pulls out his billfold, and pays money to go to a motivational program that costs $500 to $700. One young person who recognized his need for personal growth and was willing to pay the cost is a young man named Tim Carlin. Tim involved himself in Toastmasters International, which is a program I recommend for a lot of people. This program gave Tim tremendous self-confidence. As a result of his experience with Toastmasters, he is equally at ease talking with individuals or speaking before large groups. There was a time in his life when he would not have bet on having that confidence.

There are many fine motivational courses you can take. My favorite course is "The Power of Persuasion" seminar taught by Walter Hailey, Jr., of Planned Marketing Associates in Hunt, Texas. Walter is a personal friend of mine and an inspiration to me. Today, in his sixties, he has more enthusiasm than the majority of young development candidates. Walter's "boot camp" is an exciting course. You cannot complete it without knowing more about yourself and without being excited about developing your God-given talents. Anyone interested in attending his weekend course may contact our company. We'd be happy to put you in touch with him. Other outstanding speakers in the field of self-development are individuals such as Dale Carnegie, Zig Ziglar, Tony Robbins, Brian Tracy, and Dennis Waitley. You don't **have** to attend a course. You can read books, listen to audio tape programs, or watch video programs. However, I recommend attending the seminars in person. Interacting with others, seeing how others accomplish their goals, and meeting those from other career fields can be an additional source of knowledge and inspiration. Appendix A provides information about self-development programs, books, videos, and audios.

With few exceptions, the individuals I have recruited for Corporate America have been outstanding. The most dynamic and successful people find the time to grow, learn, and broaden their knowledge base. They don't allow difficult or unfortunate circumstances to prevent them from doing so. Don't waste your time or money to purchase a motivational tape or book or to attend a seminar until **you** accept the responsibility to continually re-motivate yourself for the rest of your life. Too many individuals, youth as well as adults, expect that responsibility to fall on someone else's shoulders, such as their teachers, parents, ministers, employees, or superiors. This is a very self-defeating attitude. If you find yourself locked into this kind of behavior, take charge now and take responsibility for your own motivation in life. Then, determine a course of action. You could decide to read one book a month. Or, you could listen to one motivational tape every evening as you prepare for bed, in the morning as you prepare for the day, while you exercise, or when you drive down the road. It's important to realize the constant need for self-motivation. The "real world" is tough and demanding and, in many ways, disposed to negative thinking. For proof, watch your local news tonight, read your newspaper today, or listen to your friends.

As a college student, you're going to have many people demanding your time, such as your roommates, girlfriends, boyfriends, instructors, fraternity brothers, sorority sisters, and parents. Again, you have to realize this is going to happen. Six months into college, don't say, "I'm overwhelmed by all the invitations to parties and all the functions and distractions." Wake up **now**. What are you going to do about it? Are you going to continuously be a victim of circumstance or are you going to control yourself? Why not decide early in your academic career, "Here are the things I'm going to do. Here are my priorities, my objectives. Here's how I'm going to learn how to say no." Boy, just a simple little word, **no**. Try it. Get out a tape recorder and practice saying no. "No. No. No, I don't have time. No, I have studying to do. No, I'm sorry. I have a test in three weeks, and I need to study for it. No, I'm disappointed that I can't be there, but I really have to study tonight." You'll find that when you get to college, it is much easier for you. All top students have the ability to say no. Usually, it's weaker students who can't say no. They want to please everyone. Do you know why? They have many insecurities. So, what they really want to do is have people around them at all times because that gives them confidence. That's what we would call pseudoconfidence. Prepare yourself before you go to college to say, "I'm not going to let someone else control my time." You can do it. You just have to be committed to do it and tell yourself you're going to do it before you head to the college campus.

People tell you that you should have fun when you go to college. Well, I don't disagree as long as it's after you do your homework. If someone tells you that having fun at college is more important than anything else, I'm ready to have a conversation with him or her. Just have them call me at my toll-free number. I will give a thousand reasons why that's not the frame of mind for entering college. It's always easy to have fun. It's always easy to close a book and say, "Well, I'll do it tomorrow. I don't think we'll have a pop quiz." You begin to get in the habit of procrastinating. As soon as you do that, you're setting yourself up for failure. Don't do it. Remain in control. Be tough. Be strong. That's what it takes to be successful in today's real world.

CHAPTER 2

"Graduation is the time to put your marketable skills to work — not the time to discover what they are. Roger Cameron is your most valuable source for accurate information about what skills the job market requires. Use your four years in college to apply Roger's advice which will place you head and shoulders above graduates who have failed to prepare for entering the job market."

—Laura King Elliott
Johnson & Johnson
Ethicon, Inc. Division

CHAPTER 2

Prepare For A Job During College

Getting Organized

I've never observed a highly successful person who wasn't organized. Successful people are able to juggle numerous appointments, assignments, responsibilities, and dates to remember and still meet their obligations within difficult time limits. Learning to be thoroughly organized should be part of your college education. Don't wait until others see you as unorganized and forgetful before you develop the professional habit of organizing and planning your time efficiently. I can attest to the fact that some development candidates have failed in their career for just this reason.

I strongly recommend that you purchase a planning system. Two companies that have very good ones include the following:

- Day-Timers, Inc.
  One Day-Timer Plaza
  Allentown, PA 18195-1551
  1-215-395-5884

- Franklin International Institute
  P. O. Box 31406
  Salt Lake City, UT 84131-0406
  1-800-654-1776

In addition, there are many good software programs on the market that enable you to organize using your PC. Here are a few for you to explore:

- **On Time** (Campbell Services, Inc.) — This is a DOS version that is a combination appointment book, to-do list, pocket secretary, desktop planner, tickler file, and alarm clock. It graphically illustrates allocated time and lists undated items on the to-do list.

- **On Time for Windows** (Campbell Services, Inc.) — This system has the same features as On Time for DOS except that it uses the Windows interface.

- **The DeskTop Set For Windows** (Tiger Software) — Desk Top has an address book, calendar, phone dialer, and tape calculator with pop-up menus. You can perform instant searches, import and export information, print reminders, print Rolodex cards and Day-Timer pages, create "to-do" lists, and consolidate lists into a daily prioritized list.

- **Top Priority** (Power Up Software) — This software creates task and goal lists and prints "to-do" lists and reports to fit your personal organizer. You can merge all your lists into daily "to-do" lists so that large projects and goals appear as smaller achievable tasks each day. These tasks can be imported into Calendar Creator Plus to print out a graphical calendar.

Setting Your Priorities

What then do you need to do to be prepared? First of all, you must set your priorities. Education comes before sorority or fraternity pledging, sports, class offices, working, and even dating.

Let's say you've researched the opportunities in various fields of study and have selected a major. You have a degree plan that includes the computer courses necessary to make you marketable in today's high tech world.

The next step must be to commit yourself to high GPA achievement. As we said in Chapter 1, a high GPA will give you more options in today's corporate world. Many companies establish GPA limits as pre-interview requirements. While this is a valid factor in employee selection, it is also true that companies miss some outstanding individuals who are ruled out because of lower grade point averages. However, as long as there are enough students with high GPAs to fill their needs, most companies feel that it is a justifiable loss. This is simply a matter of economics — supply and demand. Don't try to guess what the demand situation will be four years from the day you enter college. It boils down to the fact that you must take charge of your life and steer it in the direction that guarantees you will have career opportunities when you graduate.

Ask yourself what it will take to get a high GPA. There can be only one answer — your education is your first priority. As you begin your college career, think what it will mean to you four short years from now to have the GPA necessary to impress recruiters with your high achievements. It will be worth all that hard work and dedication to your education.

Hiring Tutors

One of your strategies for achieving high grades may be to hire tutors to help you with particular courses. Many students are reluctant to hire tutors. If you feel hesitant about it, measure carefully the embarrassment of hiring a tutor for a short period of time versus living with a low grade point average for the rest of your life. **I cannot encourage you enough to get help and get it fast if you have problems with particular subject matter.** While you may be able to get tutoring that is free of charge, generally speaking, a person who is being paid to tutor you is obligated to give you quality help at the time you need it and in a manner that is best for you. Your friends will have their own concerns with their own studies. Be willing to pay them if they give up time to help you. I feel strongly that it is important for you to strategize how you will handle your academic problems before you go to college. Don't wait until you're having trouble, and then make the decision to hire a tutor. Just tell yourself, "When I run into a difficulty, I am going to hire someone to help me immediately." As a matter of fact, it would be a good idea for you to set aside a fund for that purpose. React quickly when you get into that kind of situation.

Another helpful hint is to form study groups with other students. These groups can provide assistance when you are having difficulty in a subject.

Timing Is Important
If it is possible, complete your college education in a four-year period. Many of your peers are graduating at age 21, so if you're 22 at graduation, you may be considered to be a year behind, although this may be due to your birth date.

As I've said, the goal is to concentrate 100 percent of your efforts on your academics. Working during the school year may not allow you to do that, so you may have to work for a semester and then go to school. However, with a few exceptions, I like to see students accomplish their education in classic style — four years of high school, four years of college, and then start their careers. I have previously mentioned some very acceptable exceptions, such as participating in co-op programs, or studying a year and then working a year.

Planning Extracurricular Activity
Recruiters value young men and women who have demonstrated the ability to be leaders while in high school and college. Take advantage of the opportunities you have during this period to develop leadership skills. Select the organizations that interest you the most and get involved, keeping in mind the balance necessary to ensure you will be able to maintain your grades. Your contributions will establish you as a person who gets things done. Tell others of your interest in elected positions and build relationships that help you get elected. Leadership roles, such as president or vice

president of your class are well respected, as are officer positions in sororities, fraternities, academic organizations, service clubs, or honor societies. Whatever you do, do it with enthusiasm with a desire to make a contribution and to develop your leadership skills. The recognition will follow.

High school and college present you with many choices for service and social activities. Joining college social clubs is only one of those choices, but it is certainly a very popular one for many people. They offer opportunities to become well-acquainted with others, to build lasting relationships, and to develop networking and leadership skills. Before joining a social club, weigh carefully the demands it will make on your time and whether you feel you have the ability to maintain your grades and be a part of this kind of group.

If you join, you should decide from the beginning that your activity in a sorority or fraternity should be secondary to your commitment to your education. Many students allow their fraternity or sorority to be the dominant factor in their college careers. By doing this they sacrifice their future success because they are not able to maintain their grades at the same time. Know yourself. Study your assets and limitations. If you know you can handle the responsibility and still maintain a high GPA, run for leadership roles in your fraternity or sorority. These are important leadership positions. Just don't kid yourself. Being president of your sorority doesn't replace the value of high grades.

As I've said, high school and college offer many opportunities for you to donate your time to worthy causes, such as the Big Sister and Big Brother programs, the Ronald McDonald House, or the Special Olympics. These activities help you to be a more balanced, contributing person and are valued by Corporate America. Again, maintain your balance so that you don't become overwhelmed with volunteer work.

Recruiters also view leadership roles in a competitive sport as a positive indication that the experience in those roles helps students develop valuable leadership skills, which they can use in the corporate world. If you choose to be in athletics and know you can maintain your grades and spend some additional time in a leadership position, aspire to be selected by your peers as a team captain. Too often, athletes do not achieve good grades. Even if you're a world-class athlete, sports activities are not as important as academic success.

Evaluating Your Personal Habits

Take stock of your personal characteristics and how you can improve. Are you as competitive as other students? Do you have good verbal skills? Are you as poised and self-confident? Many students who go through the interview process after graduation find themselves frequently rejected. Why? Because they have no verbal enthusiasm in the interview. They are laid-back, quiet, and appear to be non-competitive. They give the recruiter the impression that they would have a hard time getting through an eight-hour workday. If others have consistently described you as quiet and unassuming, do something about it. Take self-improvement programs and work to develop strengths in your presentation style.

Many applicants tell me that when they weren't hired, they concluded they needed more education. Those students obtained their masters degree, maybe an MBA, and then went to the marketplace and still weren't hired. With all the education in the world, you still have to be able to go into an interview and convince someone that you can make a significant contribution to their company. It takes good verbal skills to persuade them of your ability to perform. You can't simply show them a resume or your sheepskin and say, "Well, I'm a college graduate. Now you can fight over me." It just doesn't happen that way. **That's not the real world.** However, I assure you that companies will fight over you if you follow the recommendations in this book. Be honest in self-appraisal. Don't make excuses for having lazy, soft verbal skills; being overweight; or having less than good grooming, proper clothing, and good posture. Think about how you appear to others. If it's not ideal, make it ideal. What a shame to work hard and get good grades and then not be hired because of poor personal habits.

Networking

Those in Corporate America have discovered the benefits of networking. Networking has become an art in itself. It involves establishing and maintaining relationships with people. It doesn't just happen. You must work at it. As a student, you may know individuals in the corporate world — or you may not. You will find that most people enjoy helping students direct their careers and will talk to you and give you information. It's up to you to make the contacts. Look for opportunities with everyone you meet to develop relationships and to gather information on available jobs in their industries or companies.

During college observe other outstanding students. Make their acquaintance, develop friendships, and, most of all, maintain those friendships. Remember the law of maintaining relationships: You must give as much or more than you receive. Think about what you have to offer other people that will contribute real value to their lives, and develop those capabilities. Too many people wait too late in life to appreciate the value of developing good relationships with others. I would suggest you develop your network in many different career paths, such as engineering, finance, data processing, accounting, and manufacturing. At any time in your career, you should be able to telephone a close friend who is employed as an engineer to discuss a technical issue or to call someone in finance to talk about financial analysis or financial planning for the future.

Developing A Master Mind Group

Another excellent way to network is to form a "master mind" group. Many executives and entrepreneurs are members of master mind groups. Members meet periodically to brainstorm solutions to issues of importance to them. The master mind principle makes it possible for an individual, through association with others, to acquire the knowledge of those individuals without having their education level. For example, an engineer can explain a technical principle perfectly, but you don't need a four-year engineering degree to understand it. The master mind concept suggests that there is more opportunity for success in dealing with obstacles to a goal if two or more minds work in perfect harmony toward that goal.

Scarcely a day goes by that we aren't gaining information from diverse, educated, and knowledgeable people, and understanding it — without an equal amount of education. Most of us go through life having non-formal master mind alliances, usually in an unconscious state of mind. I'm suggesting you formalize your own master mind group.

I belong to two master mind groups. I regret waiting until I was 55 years old to become a member. I have received many direct benefits, allowing me to save many hours of frustration and to accomplish some personal goals more quickly and more efficiently. I hope, at the same time, I have contributed to others in my groups. Don't put the master mind idea on a back burner. Take advantage of the synergy gained from such an alliance.

One of the major goals of a college master mind group should be to help the members do as much as possible to improve their opportunities to have successful careers. For example, your group will want to address specific career opportunities in your field and discuss how members of the group can achieve higher performance in school.

Be selective about who will be a member of your group. Choose people with similar interests, who have the intelligence and enthusiasm to contribute significantly to the group, and who have been successful in the past. Select people from all areas of the campus. Friends may or may not be appropriate choices. Consider inviting recent alumni from your college who have worked in Corporate America for a year or two to be members, keeping in mind that those individuals must see some value in being part of the group.

> **Early in your career, it is what you know;**
> **then, it becomes who you know;**
> **finally, it changes to who knows you.**

While it is important to join business fraternities on your campus that relate to your field of study, a master mind group can be a valuable method of developing the business contacts and information you need as well. Sometimes business fraternities become only social outlets and do not provide the opportunities for you to make business contacts or find the solutions to challenges through a vigorous exchange of ideas.

Your group may want to invite people in your majors to speak on topics of importance to you and, afterwards, to answer questions from the group. Consider pooling resources and hiring training consultants who deliver business seminars to instruct your group. The opportunities are endless. The point is that as a group you have some exciting ideas to explore.

If, for some reason, an individual does not fit in the group, be firm about asking the individual to drop his membership. The key is to have an extremely compatible, supportive group with members who are enthusiastic about meeting the objectives of the group.

If you are the leader of the group, be sure to maintain a positive attitude at all times. Your responsibility is to help the other members maintain a lively interest in being supportive and cooperative.

Your group can be as large or as small as you like. The larger the group, the longer you need to meet so that everyone can have time to contribute. Establish a specific time each week or every two weeks for the meeting. Students have busy schedules during the day. Trying to set up meetings during this time will be difficult. Try early morning (6:30 a.m.) or late in the evening (9:30 p.m.) when most of the members might be able to attend.

Considering Other Employment Opportunities

If you graduate with an MBA, you have the opportunity to consider participation in the MBA Enterprise Corps, headquartered at the University of North Carolina in Chapel Hill. This is a program that finds positions in Eastern European countries for business school graduates from a consortium of 16 U.S. schools. Salaries for these positions are considered to be "subsistence level." However, the long-term benefits could be worth the experience. For example, think about the benefit to an MBA graduate whose long-term goals are international management. Her assignment is to work in Krakow, Poland as a consultant in finance, possibly to help with their privatization efforts. Given her goals, this experience will be extremely valuable.

If you think your long-term goals would be served by participation in a program of this type, ask counselors in your school for information.

Searching The Market

As a result of networking with family, friends, and business acquaintances through your individual efforts, as well as your participation in business fraternities and a master mind group, you probably have generated some job opportunities. Additionally, you should attend career conferences and job fairs presented by consortiums of companies or by recruiters, register with your school's job referral office and work with them to set up interviews, and read and respond to classified ads.

When should you be actively pursuing a position? As we have suggested, networking and participation in a master mind group are two activities you can begin early in your college career. You should be steadily developing your contacts so that you are building relationships to help you step smoothly from school into the corporate world.

During your junior year, talk to your school's job referral office. Discuss your major and interests with a counselor and ask for the office's help in determining how you should strategize to get the most from their service. Ask them for the names of companies that have positions in your field and will be interviewing on campus. Find out exactly when recruiters from these companies will be interviewing. Determine when you must have a resume prepared for the school, what the qualifications are for the companies who are interviewing, and when you must sign up for the interviews. Mark your calendar and make this a Number 1 Priority! In the interim before your interviews, research the companies extensively at your library and write or call their public relations offices for annual reports and other company literature. If you don't know how to find information about companies at your school library, ask the reference librarian for assistance.

The next chapter discusses how to produce a resume that makes that all-important first impression with a dynamite presentation of you, your skills, and your accomplishments.

CHAPTER 3

"I wish I had read *Your Career Fast Track* early in my academic career and used Roger's time-proven guidelines to help make the many difficult decisions that exist from high school through college and into the business world. Read, learn, and put into practice Roger's formula for success."

—Chuck Alvarez
Becton-Dickinson, Inc.

CHAPTER 3

Create The Crucial First Impression

What is the **first impression** you make to a prospective employer? In the thousands of speeches I've given around the world, I've often asked my audiences this question. I haven't yet heard the answer I believe is the correct one. People say it's the appearance you make as you step into the recruiter's office: your suit, your dress, your grooming, the sparkle in your eyes, your voice inflection, your walk, or your handshake. I emphatically believe all these factors make up the **second** impression.

The first impression is your **resume** or **application.** Ninety-nine percent of the time, the resume is seen even before an application.

**POOR RESUMES/POOR
APPLICATIONS = DECLINE**

As recruiters evaluate your resume, they get an impression about you. It can be one of tremendous interest — or of no interest at all. Let's focus on what a resume should do for you.

WRITING A RESUME: THE VITAL INFORMATION

Availability Date

I have yet to receive a resume with the date the applicant will be available on it. I always ask applicants when they are available. First and foremost, a resume should tell a recruiter your date of availability. A position is open. The date you are available should coincide with that position being open or when the position **will** be open. You may be the best applicant going — but, if your availability doesn't coincide with the appropriate time for the company, then you're of no value to that company.

Level Of Education

Second, show your level of education. It's important because jobs often call for specific educational background. If your education isn't appropriate for the position, the corporation needs to know early in the process.

Accomplishments

In your resume, include significant accomplishments you have made. Corporate America judges success by the degree of **difficulty** of the objectives for the accomplishments. Employers are looking for individuals who have already demonstrated they can handle difficult projects and successfully complete them. They are not so interested in knowing that you completed a task within a tight timeframe (although it is important to be able to meet deadlines) but, rather, that the responsibility you had was a difficult one.

> **Some objectives are more difficult to achieve than others and, therefore, are more significant successes when accomplished.**

For example, let's say your sorority initiated a fund-raising campaign for a local charity, and you were the chairman of the fund-raising committee. Historically, raising funds on the campus or in the college town in which your school is located had been very difficult. In addition, the economy in the town was very depressed. However, you set a high goal, energized your sorority members, established alliances on campus with other organizations for support, and managed to exceed the goal while maintaining a 3.7 GPA.

Recently, an applicant asked me to evaluate his resume. I pointed out to him that he had failed to provide quantified accomplishments. What he had done was to state that he had a GPA of 3.74, thus saying to the recruiter that he felt it was important for him to know how well he had done. He quantified his success academically and showed the importance of quantifying his accomplishment. However, he never quantified his success in his work experience or extracurricular activities. Realize that being a member of an organization does not mean you contributed to that organization. Being president of an organization does not mean you successfully improved on your club's objectives. Don't assume that your resume will adequately represent your level of contribution to an organization just because you specify your membership or position as an officer in that organization. The individuals reading it will not necessarily infer that you were a successful contributor.

When providing your accomplishments, think about the difficulty of the objective and the degree to which you succeeded in accomplishing the objective. State the degree of success in your description of the accomplishment. For example, let's say you worked in a deli in high school and were asked to reduce the waste produced in cutting meat. Your description might be stated like this: "Recommended improved methods of operation and maintenance of meat-slicing equipment that reduced the waste associated with meat slicing by 90 percent. (Notice that a percentage that indicates the degree of success is stated.) Or, let's say you worked as a receptionist for a large office that required a hand-written log of inventory. You spent at least 10 hours a month inventorying supplies. Because of your computer knowledge, you knew a lot about database programs and saw an opportunity to reduce the amount of time required in this activity. As a result of your initiative in recommending and teaching others how to use the program, the time spent in checking inventory was reduced to five hours a month.

Stating Your Objective

Your resume should include your career **objective.** It must be very specific and to the point, such as: "Position in sales leading to management (*or* in management information systems *or* in line operations *or* in staff engineering *or* in manufacturing *or* in operations). A stated objective on the resume helps the recruiter to do two things: 1) determine whether the company has an opening that matches your interests; and 2) verify that you are directed in your career search and self-confident enough to say so. Most corporate recruiters are interested in students who have predetermined what careers best suit their interests and skills and who have confidence they can achieve what they want.

When you set up interviews with your college placement center, they may give you different instructions about stating objectives. Often, placement centers have agreements with companies that all resume objectives will be broad-based, allowing students to maximize their breadth of interviewing. Therefore, the recruiters will not penalize you for your objective. However, in a situation in which you send your resume to a company as an individual not affiliated with a placement center, a broad-based objective is not in your best interest. It may give a recruiter cause to eliminate you from consideration.

Students frequently state in their objectives that they want to start in a management position (either mid-level, lower mid-level, upper mid-level, or entry-level). I recommend that you say "supervisory — leading to management" position instead. The words, "position in management," eliminate you from many top companies because these companies develop management from within.

In the many years I have recruited, I have never placed anyone in a "management" role. Managers set big picture objectives; supervisors motivate subordinates to carry out those objectives. The companies I represent promote management from internal personnel. The reason is clear. Companies have a morale problem when they hire management from outside the company. Imagine yourself working for a company for a four- or five-year period of time, finding a management spot opening up above you, and then seeing the company hire someone from the outside for that position. You would be very unhappy and demoralized. So, state on your resume that you want a supervisory position instead. You will find it will be read, and the odds for pursuit will increase.

Supporting The Primary Objective

When you list your accomplishments on your resume, be sure they **support the primary objective** of the position you held. This is critical.

If you expect to be hired as a supervisor in Corporate America, then you should highlight your accomplishments based on your supervisory experience. Tell about your successes in motivating peers or subordinates. If you worked at a McDonald's Restaurant and were promoted to shift supervisor, you need to talk about your successes in motivating others. If you were elected to a leadership role — such as president of your class, sorority, or fraternity — you can draw on these experiences to show your ability to motivate. Emphasize two considerations in motivating: keeping turnover low and morale high. Quantify your accomplishment. For example, as president of your sorority, let's say you increased members' participation in campus honorary societies by encouraging higher

GPAs. Your description of the accomplishment might be: "Managed an initiative to increase members' participation in honorary societies. Ten members out of 30 increased their GPAs sufficiently to join honorary societies. Members enthusiastically endorsed the activity."

If your primary job objective is an engineering position, then show the recruiter your accomplishments in engineering. These accomplishments might come from participation in a co-op program, a science project, work, or even a hobby. Always remember that your accomplishments must draw as close a parallel as possible to the position for which you are interviewing. It's fine to list collateral successes, but they should be secondary on a resume.

Quantifying Your Successes
Recognize that corporations are looking at how actions affect the bottom line. They are interested in how to increase profitability, decrease costs, and increase productivity. Learn their language. They are looking for quantification on your resume. For example, let's say that during college you were the chairman of an organization that conducted fund-raising for the homeless. If you reached your goal and even exceeded it, let us know this was, for example, three percent above objective. Unfortunately, many students don't understand the importance of quantifying their accomplishments. They tell how they developed a program without telling exactly what the program accomplished.

Applicants have told me, "But, Roger, I paid a resume service $75 to get this resume produced." I may step on toes here, but too many times resume services do not provide the expertise required to project the right concepts to Corporate America. Without this expertise their interest is in making the resume look pretty. I maintain that if resume services charged you according to the **success** the resume produces (or fails to produce), they might be more serious about what the resume says.

It is better to build two, three, or even four different resumes based on different objectives than to have one resume with an objective that attempts to cover everything.

Your resume must represent bottom line qualities and **attract** a company to you.

Common Misconceptions

Most students want to build a one-page resume. I agree with this. Most of you will have limited experience by your senior year. However, if you have worked your way through college or are a co-op student and have significant accomplishments, do **not** be concerned about having a two-page resume.

Many applicants also feel their resumes should be on the best bond paper. I agree. But the **content** is what's important. I've had recruiters tell me, "I don't care if they write it on paper grocery bags, as long as the content is right and we can get the information we need."

The resume format I recommend is based on the years I've spent recruiting entry-level development candidates and working daily with companies. I have asked these firms what they want to see in a resume to obtain the information they need. I want to note here that I have been in a business where I am paid only for bottom-line performance, not for my opinion. This fact should lend credibility to this resume format.

This format reflects the feelings of some of the top corporate recruiters in America. They told me exactly what they needed to know — and what format to use.

Most resumes should be held to one page. But don't be afraid to go beyond that, providing the information is relevant and presented in an articulate, succinct manner.

Resume Format Suggestions

Be careful and thorough. Follow these specific instructions in preparing your resume.

- The **appearance** should be as follows:
  - Use plain paper, measuring 8 1/2 by 11 inches.
  - Use 1/2-inch margins for each side.
  - Begin 3/4 to 1 inch from the top of the page on page one.
  - Begin 1 inch from the top on page two. On the first line, type your name. On the second line, type "Page 2 continued." Both lines should be flush right.
  - Drop down three lines to begin the body of your resume, using the same 1/2-inch margins.
  - Leave 1/2 inch to 1 inch at the bottom of each page.
  - Keep your resume to one or two pages.

- The **body** of your resume should contain the following information:
  - **Personal information:** Full name, address, home phone number, marital status. Additionally, consider adding your age, height, and weight when they are ideal. While it may be illegal for a company to ask for some of this information, it is not illegal for you to volunteer it. It wasn't Corporate America that made the decision that they didn't want this data. It was our government that said we can't discriminate on that basis. I do not disagree with this requirement, but at the same time, whenever you have information that will put you in a better position, by all means give it. Companies will be more likely to pursue the resume that gives them the information they desire.

  - **Date of availability:** Availability is extremely critical. Give a firm date. Some jobs simply cannot wait forever. Put yourself in the position of company recruiters. They get many resumes every day and are going to pick up the resumes that disclose all the information.

- **Education information**: Degrees attained, year graduated, high school and college activities, scholastic honors, offices held, and athletic activities.

- **Experience**: Dates and titles of positions held, specific responsibilities, and two to four accomplishments per job. If you're interviewing for sales or manufacturing leadership positions, focus on accomplishments that emphasize your skills in working with and leading people. If you have a technical background, include any technical experience you may have. Don't generalize this information or water it down. Be specific. See Appendix F for a sample resume format.

The Cover Letter

If you mail your resume, it is crucial to send a cover letter. You might also consider including a cover letter with your resume even if you're handing it to someone. The letter must be written specifically to that company. Do not send generic cover letters. You're telling the company all they need to know to decline you. Don't be lazy in developing either of these documents.

The resume must be able to stand on its own. Often, your cover letter will be removed from the resume as it is forwarded to hiring managers, and the managers will be unaware of it. If you have put important information in this letter which is not on your resume, it's likely to stay with the personnel director to whom you addressed it.

Make powerful statements in the cover letter. What can you offer that is relevant to that particular company? What are your skills, experiences, abilities, and career accomplishments? Why do you have a real interest in this corporation? For example: "I'm particularly interested in your company because it is No. 1 in your industry with a 21 percent market share. I was also impressed by the statement made by your president that 'service to your customers will come before profit' and that every employee of the company must be responsible for product quality. Your company is exactly the type I respect and want to work for."

I consider your resume to be one of the most critical aspects of your job search. It's the primary factor, so do it first. You must have **documentation** on paper, listing who you are and what skills and experience you have, including your past performance. I find that too many students spend very little time on their resumes. What they produce simply isn't enough.

When you walk through the door for an interview, you want to know that you're in front of a recruiter who, through reading your resume, already has a very positive attitude about you.

Getting The Interview

Let's say you have the best resume you can produce and you have written cover letters specific to the companies with which you want to interview. Once you have sent the resumes, mark your calendar to make follow-up telephone calls within a week. Then, be sure you make them.

Don't hesitate to be professionally assertive in presenting yourself and your qualifications. For example, consider making an unsolicited call to a company's recruiting office to present your resume. Personnel in recruiting offices often "spot" for recruiters and give good reports of individuals who appear to be outstanding candidates for jobs. Consider asking for the recruiter and presenting your resume in person as well. On occasion you may have friends, family, or associates who work in an organization that is advertising an opening in which you are interested. Ask them to find out who the manager is for that position, present your resume, and then recommend you as a person to consider. A referral from an employee of a company may give you a better opportunity to get an interview than if you send or present your resume to the personnel office. When you ask your friends to recommend you, be certain you are asking them to assist you in getting an interview rather than to help you get **hired**.

The next chapter gives you specific information about how to interview — a very critical activity in the process and one for which quality preparation is essential!

APPLICATION

Your application to a company (the actual application form) is a document that will represent you for the balance of your career if you go to work for that company. **Think about that.** It must be filled out in a manner that would represent you personally in your permanent records.

This form may be the first impression a company representative has of you. Don't underestimate its importance. Think carefully as you complete the basic form.

Follow these basic rules:

1) **Carefully** follow the specific instructions, such as "Print" or "List last position first."

2) Always type the application whenever possible. If you choose to handwrite, print the information in a neat, legible hand. Always use dark ink, preferably black. There should be no mark-outs. A small amount of correcting fluid is acceptable, but correction tape is not.

3) Use a dictionary to check for correct **spelling** and a grammar book for correct **punctuation and grammar**.

4) Don't leave blanks. If a question doesn't apply to you, put a short dash in the space and write "None" or "N/A" (Not Applicable). **Complete the entire form**; don't skip questions.

5) Try to fill in the entire space provided for an answer. For example, if there are three lines to list school activities, fill in all three lines.

6) Never put "See Resume." The company representative knows he can look at your resume. Put all the information **where the company wants it:** on the application.

7) Avoid attaching an addendum, or additional sheet. Although a form may state, "Feel free to attach supplemental information," the attached sheet can become detached, and then vital information will be lost. If there are four spaces provided for work history and you had six jobs, use two of the spaces for two jobs each. Your entire background should be divided so that all your positions are included in the spaces provided. **Do not** use just one space to indicate several years of job experience and then the remaining three spaces for less notable work.

8) If asked to state "Reason for seeking change" or "Reason for leaving" a past or a present position, **do** give an answer. However, your reason for leaving your position should be carefully worded. If it was a summer job, state it as such.

You'll find three **caution areas** on many applications. These are especially sensitive subjects. Here is how to deal with them.

* **Salary**. Answer "Open or negotiable." Please note this is **not** the way you would handle this question in an interview itself, but an application cannot elaborate. It can't modify. You don't dare allow the application to get you ruled out because you

supplied a figure that doesn't allow identification based upon circumstance. "Open or negotiable" allows you to discuss the entire subject of compensation in person with the company representative. It indicates salary is just one of many items you will consider when making a career decision.

- **Location.** Always state "Open" on the application. **Again, this is completely different from what you should do in the interview itself.** If the word "open" is used in an interview, it will frequently get you ruled out. If this question has two parts — "Do you have a preference?" and "Do you have any restrictions?" — answer the first by stating a broad geographical preference, such as "the Northeast," "the Southern United States," or "east of the Mississippi River." Answer the second question "None." If you know the location of the job for which you're interviewing, you can tailor your answer to that area. For example, you can state a preference of "east of the Mississippi" with "no" restrictions. National companies hire people they can promote without severe geographical restrictions.

- **Position Desired/Objective.** Always **state precisely** the position title/objective. State only **one** objective per application, even if the application provides space for more than one position title.

Many applications cause me to decline an applicant immediately. I say to myself, "I don't even want to take the time to type a rejection letter, put a stamp on it, and mail it. This file doesn't warrant taking my time." But because I feel it is my professional responsibility, I do it anyway. Sloppy applications could misrepresent the applicants. On the other hand, they may not!

In summary, the application is tangible, permanent evidence of your ability to answer specific questions and organize your ideas accurately and concisely.

Part II: Interviewing Techniques

CHAPTER 4

"*Your Career Fast Track* is experienced, candid, and valuable advice from someone who knows the hiring process of Corporate America. Maybe this is not what the passive job seeker wants to hear, because Mr. Cameron does not 'pull any punches' about preparation and practice. The sections on interviewing are particularly powerful and useful."

—Arden Showalter, Director
Career Center
Southern Methodist University

CHAPTER 4 ==========

Prepare For The Interview

What makes successful interviewing? That's simple — **preparation.** Preparation includes:
- A thorough understanding of yourself.
- An analysis of what has made you successful.
- The ability to communicate those successes in a persuasive manner.

Sounds easy, doesn't it? But it isn't. Many applicants feel they have the ability to take any subject matter and speak about it off the cuff in an articulate, concise, and convincing manner. Unfortunately, few actually can. As a matter of fact, I'm not sure I've ever met anyone during my recruiting career who got a job without interview preparation. Corporate recruiters are adamant that applicants prepare well for interviewing. They feel that if applicants do not work hard to prepare for something as valuable as their own career, then why should any company believe they're going to work hard to accomplish an objective for their employer. I think this correlation is a very accurate one.

Dedicate time to prepare for the interview. Set aside a specific period of time — an hour a day, two hours a day, five hours a week, one-half day a week, Saturday morning, Sunday afternoon — well in advance of interviews with corporate recruiters. Find the time it takes to read books, to do work assignments, and to prepare for the key questions you know will be asked. I often use this example: You wouldn't play a championship game on Saturday and take the prior week off. If you did, you certainly know what the outcome would be. As a matter of fact, you would probably work twice as hard practicing the week before.

I've talked to many applicants who interviewed with Corporate America without adequate preparation and never received offers. Consequently, without really wanting to, they took their careers in different directions. I honestly believe that, in many cases, they were rejected by Corporate America not because of their credentials, but because of their inability to **communicate** those credentials. It would be nice if you could be hired on the basis of a resume or an application. But it's just not possible. I've never known one of my client companies to hire an applicant sight unseen. So, dedicate time and energy to preparation for a very difficult venture — interviewing.

Starting With A Proper Frame Of Mind

The purpose of interviewing, getting started in a career, or changing jobs is to fulfill personal objectives. However, when you interview you must put the needs of the employer above your own. Most applicants don't do this but instead view interviews from a purely selfish perspective. They think only about what the company or job can give them — money, location, ideal jobs at all times, recognition, promotion, and benefits. While it is natural to be intensely interested in what you can get from a job, it is also costly to have a recruiter perceive this selfish perspective.

To be in the proper frame of mind for an interview, concentrate solely on the value, skills, and experience you bring to a company that enable you to contribute significantly to its objectives. If you'll use this philosophy not only in your preparation for interviews but also throughout your life experiences, you'll be rewarded with great riches, whatever you determine them to be. I firmly believe the adage, "The more you help others get what they want, the more you'll get what you want."

Objective/Subjective Assets

Objective and subjective assets are important for you to understand as you prepare for interviewing. Highlight or flag this section so that when you begin actual preparation, you'll start with this topic.

When I ask applicants during the interview process what objective assets they will bring to an employer on the first day, they frequently have no answer. You will be asked this question in one form or another. It's important for you to understand the concepts, so you can reply intelligently.

The cornerstone of self-evaluation is to understand objective and subjective assets. An objective asset is one that makes a point of fact. On the other hand, a subjective asset is a conditional value, one that is a matter of opinion.

In the interviewing context, you bring a company certain objective assets that are non-debatable, such as academic degrees or leadership experiences. The requirements for objective assets may change from interview to interview, depending on the needs of the interviewing company. As we have said, subjective assets are a matter of opinion or interpretation. They are characteristics, competencies, or behavioral traits, such as poise, self-confidence, good organizational skills, or an aptitude for hard work.

For an asset to become an objective value, it must be **required** by the employer. For example, let's say Company XYZ calls me to recruit engineers with leadership experience. In essence Company XYZ is stating that "objectively speaking" applicants must have an engineering degree and leadership experience to interview with them. These two required assets are an objective **value** to Company XYZ. In addition to these two required assets, Company XYZ states strong computer literacy will be helpful but not required. If you have an engineering degree and leadership experience, you have the objective assets required to interview with Company XYZ. Now, let's say you are very computer literate, but your skills are not comparable to those of a computer science major. Your computer literacy will be considered **objective value-added.** If you have an MBA, but it is not required, it will be considered additional objective value-added. And if you're a minority, but this is not required, your minority status will also be considered additional objective value-added. Realize that what is value-added for one company may be required by another.

Let's consider this scenario: Ms. Hildebrand from ABC, Inc. calls to ask me to recruit development candidates for her. My first question is, "What are you looking for?" She says, "Roger, I want **business-degreed** students with **GPAs of 3.0 or above**—individuals who have participated in **varsity sports** or **elected leadership roles** and who are able to start to work by **September 15**." If you have these objective assets, you now have the qualifications to interview with ABC, Inc. Ms. Hildebrand then states she would like to tell me about the subjective assets her company **values**. She says, "We're looking for individuals with strong work ethics. I want people who are willing to work hard to earn their pay. We insist on goal-oriented, make-it-happen types." Ms. Hildebrand explains goal-oriented means the willingness to establish or accept high goals that are difficult — but, more importantly, the discipline to **fight** through **adversity** to accomplish those goals. In addition, her company wants people who are team players; who are creative, innovative thinkers; who have vision; and who have pleasant personalities. This scenario is just one example. You can imagine the wide variations of subjective values that different companies look for.

To prepare for the interview process, first list all the objective assets you possess that might be of value to companies. Stretch your imagination! I've been given unique requirements over the years. For instance, I once was told by a company that they needed applicants with 3.0 GPAs or higher who had lived in the South and were six feet tall or taller! The last two requirements could be considered unusual — but requirements nonetheless. Remember that if an asset is **required**, it becomes an objective value. Once you have closely analyzed your objective assets, you must determine those the company wants so that in an interview you can stress the specific assets that are of value to the company. There is never time in any interview for you to cover everything, and there is no reason to discuss assets that are not of value to the company. Sometimes job descriptions state objective assets very clearly, and at other times you will have to be very creative to uncover this information.

It's important for you to realize that for most positions your **objective** assets determine your **functional** value to Corporate America. For these positions, your objective assets actually get you in the door and allow you to interview. Therefore, by being conscious of this early in your college career, you can work harder to establish as many objective assets as possible. Some of these objective assets will be value-added, depending on the organizations. The more assets you have, the broader your marketability. It's really pretty simple. The more objective assets you have, the more recruiters to which you will appeal and the more doors of opportunity that will be open to you.

Exceptions to this rule are sales positions that may require no objective value. In other words, the academic degree you have is immaterial. It could be any degree. In fact, the recruiter may not even bother with objective value but will concentrate only on your subjective assets. For some sales positions, a particular degree is important to have — for instance, when the product is very technical. In those cases, a corresponding technical degree is required. It would then be necessary for you to have an objective asset (technical degree, for example) before you could interview with the company.

Do you realize some of your classmates may spend four years in college and graduate with **no** objective assets? I don't think they will do this on purpose. Rather, I think they lack adequate planning and knowledge. If you want broad marketability when you graduate, be sure you have built your **objective** net worth.

While objective assets will get you in the door, **subjective assets will get you hired.** Therefore, your preparation for interviews should also include analysis of your subjective assets and practice in articulating them. You need to be able to describe as many of your subjective assets as you can with examples of accomplishments that required these assets. Therefore, after you have analyzed and listed your objective assets, make a list of your subjective assets. What do you consider to be your strengths and distinguishing characteristics? As you make your list, think in terms of what is most important to recruiters. (There are certain assets that many companies look for in applicants, such as initiative, creativity, ability to be innovative, enthusiasm, goal orientation, ability to be a team player, conceptual and analytical skills, communication skills, and interpersonal skills.)

Next, take what you feel are your most important five or six subjective assets and practice illustrating them in your answers to interviewing questions such as, "Tell me about a significant problem and **how** you solved it," or "Tell me about a significant accomplishment and **how** you accomplished it." Speak into a tape recorder and have someone else listen to the tape to determine how you illustrated your assets. If **they** can't hear them in your answers without you actually pointing them out, a recruiter won't hear them either.

Remember to **be yourself** in interviews. Your experiences are **your** experiences. If you think them through now and in depth, you will be able to clearly discuss them in interviews. Recruiters will see your strengths and be able to determine how well you fit their companies.

Recruiters expect you to verbally create a scenario that **illustrates** your assets. By doing this you maintain your individuality. If everyone simply listed these assets, they would all sound alike. The foundation of a successful interview is knowing what your subjective and objective assets are. After all, if you don't have good "product" knowledge, you will have a hard time selling the "product" — yourself.

Two Categories Of Your Life

Many applicants fail in the interview because they focus only on their four years in college. However, recruiters evaluate your high school and college achievements **equally**. **Equally** is the key word. First, we evaluate high school academic records based on quantifiable factors: the grade point average, the size of your class, your ranking within that class, your choice of curriculum, the degree of difficulty of the curriculum, and if you were in honors programs. Then, we look at extracurricular activities. What did you do outside academics? We determine whether you were elected to leadership roles by your peers or superiors. We also examine your work record to identify the beginning of a positive work ethic.

After looking at your high school accomplishments, we evaluate your college years. We cover the same areas and questions used in evaluating high school information, but we add two critical factors — the quality of your college and the quality of your curriculum.

Next, we investigate what you have done outside college to determine if you are a person who constantly strives to grow. We are interested in people who have developed outside interests, and it doesn't matter to us what they are. We don't care whether it's running, hiking, handball, family outings, reading, flying, boating, camping, Boy Scouts, Girl Scouts, Big Brothers, or any other interesting pursuit. We like to see a diversity of activities. We're not looking for carbon copies.

We are also interested in the fact that if you're married, you have a good marriage — that if you have a family, you have a good family life. However, these are illegal interview questions that we can't ask you. Consider the fact that recruiters may receive this kind of information from other applicants. Since a stable marriage and family life are positive factors for a recruiter to think about in making a decision regarding an applicant, you may want to consider sharing this information.

A very important part of our evaluation is to determine how poised and self-confident you are. This is the conversational portion of the interview. This is important because you will be placed in a new environment and will be expected to achieve a variety of objectives and make a positive contribution to profitability immediately. Your employer will be evaluating your ability to make significant accomplishments early in your career. You must have the poise and confidence to move into an unknown situation and perform immediately. While it is true that most of this is subjective in the interview, we can determine it by your ability to:

- Communicate easily without showing signs of nervousness.
- Use first names in a natural manner.
- Develop instant rapport.
- Demonstrate good self-insight and a willingness to openly discuss your strengths and weaknesses.

You must communicate well so you can make a positive contribution in as short a period of time as possible. Corporate America cannot mandate that you work well with other people. You can get up and walk out the door any time you want. So, it is important for us to hire people with professional quality — people who work well with others and are eager to come to work each morning. Corporations are not looking for the cocky person whose self-confidence controls them. They want people who have total control of their self-confidence and who know they're good but don't have to wear it on their sleeve or act as if they're the best. As I interview around the world, it's interesting to find that the really good people do not have to inflate the numbers. They are not afraid to tell us that they're a 7 on a scale of 10 in leadership style, that they're an 8 in computer science, or that they're a 5 and lack hands-on mechanical experience. Only those who lack self-confidence feel they must tell me they're a 10 in everything they do. Realize a 10 claims that he/she is perfect, and there is no room for growth. Quality people always **admit** to having more room to grow. We want people who have good self-insight — who feel comfortable with themselves and can honestly identify their strengths and weaknesses. They want a company to hire them on the basis of what they are, not what they can pretend to be in an interview or in a series of interviews.

Do we always get the ideal candidate? I probably never have. In evaluating applicants, I put the positives on one scale and the negatives on the other. However, I do expect the positive side of the scale to crash to the floor. That's the kind of person corporations want and are going to hire.

Applicants have told me they're not sure whether they want a career in the profit-oriented world or in civil service. Can you imagine a company saying, "Roger, we want you to find us an individual who is uncertain about a career in the profit-oriented world?" Profit and non-profit philosophies are diametrically opposed. Corporations are looking for people who have a burning desire to get involved in Corporate America and rise to the top. We're looking for **capitalists**. We must **see** that desire.

If an applicant says, "Several years down the road, I want to own my own business," I have to rule out that applicant. You wouldn't want someone to walk into your place of business and say, "I want you to train me, develop me, and pay me a high salary. Then, I can save money, go across the street, open my own business, and go into competition with you."

I'm not asking you to be dishonest. I am asking you to evaluate what you want to do with your life. If it is to establish your own business, I respect that. (After all, I own my own business.) But, don't use somebody else to do it. Just do the necessary preparatory work, open your business, and be successful. If you want a career in Corporate America, then commit to that goal. Take advantage of every opportunity for development that a company offers to help you go to the top. Be a leader within that company. I grant you things will change in the future. There are curves in every road, but to start a developmental career with a company, knowing you're going to leave in the near future, is unprofessional and dishonest.

Developing Self-Insight

Corporate recruiters frequently ask me to bring them people who have the ability to analyze their skills realistically and to present themselves self-confidently. There must be a balance between being realistic and being self-confident. One applicant who interviewed with me had not developed the insight to be able to do this. On his application for a position, he stated that he wanted to be CEO — a very lofty goal. My responsibility was to determine if he had evidence that he could accomplish the objective.

I reviewed his high school records to see how many times he had been number one. He hadn't graduated from high school as number one. He had a 3.1 GPA. Nor had he been elected to leadership roles. In college his GPA was 2.7. He had not been elected to class president, student body president, or, for that matter, team captain of any athletic sport. Because his record could not support his objective, I had to decline his application for the position. This individual stated that he felt I was communicating that he should not have high goals. I told him he misunderstood my position; that he **should** have high goals — goals that made him perspire, goals that used every asset he possessed to accomplish them — but that those goals also had to be realistic. In this case, becoming CEO could have been a personal goal, but it should never have appeared on his application. It is important for you to have high goals, but be totally objective about your ability to achieve them. Don't automatically set yourself up for failure.

Most applicants feel it necessary to say they are 9s or 10s in everything they do. Again, be realistic. We recruit students from college campuses such as Harvard, Wharton, Stanford, Northwestern, Duke, and other top schools across the country. Recruiters for Corporate America are accustomed to having the very best. You will be compared with people who are graduating from top schools with excellent GPAs. We know you have a great ability to perform, but we want you to realize exactly who you are and what your value is to Corporate America. You will interview with some of the best-managed companies in America. They can only apply their management expertise to you if you admit there are areas in which you can improve. Don't shut off this great asset by suggesting you have little or no room to grow. **I can't count the number of applicants I've seen rejected because of inflated self-esteem.**

Covering Your Weaknesses
Many students want to talk only about their strengths. However, recruiters want to talk about their weaknesses, and applicants haven't prepared themselves to discuss this topic. Great marketing companies in America have taught their sales people how to present product weaknesses so they do not outweigh the strengths. Communicating your weaknesses improperly will cause you to be ruled out of an interview.

One way to think about weaknesses is to analyze your strengths in relation to others. As you can see in the graph below, there are two strength lines: your normal strength line and your age group strength line. Your normal strength line is higher than the strength line for most people in your age group. There are those in your age group who did not finish high school, did not attend college, and have not had quality successes. The graph illustrates that any characteristic you would describe as "less than a strength" still would not qualify as a "weakness" as it would for most people in your age group. Those characteristics that are described as "less than a strength" are those that do not cause us to fail in the accomplishment of an objective. Unfortunately, recruiters won't ask you for "a less than a strength" even though that is really what they are looking for. After all, if you have a consistent weakness, do you really think they will hire you?

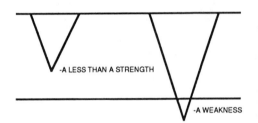

YOUR NORMAL STRENGTH LINE

-A LESS THAN A STRENGTH

AGE GROUP STRENGTH LINE

-A WEAKNESS

Now, how do you answer the question, "What are your weaknesses?" First, be honest. If you truly have a weakness, state it but with qualifiers, such as "on rare occasions," "very seldom," "now and then," "rarely," and "once and a while." For example, if you feel you have an occasional problem managing time efficiently, you could say, "I like managing my time efficiently, have a great organizer system, and feel I organize my time well. However, I can specifically remember a couple of situations during my four years in college that could have been more efficiently managed." You've been candid but, in reality, have described an occasional "less than a strength" as a weakness. By using the strong qualifiers we suggest, you are leaving an important impression — that your weaknesses "rarely" or "seldom" present a challenge to the achievement of your objectives. Again, the key in describing weaknesses (less than strengths) is to emphasize the fact that you experience them very infrequently.

In addition to using qualifiers to modify a weakness, identify specifically what you are doing to overcome the weakness. Using the example of a weakness in time management, you could suggest a definite process you have established to ensure good planning. You might say, "I can specifically remember a couple of situations during my four years in college that could have been more efficiently managed. Now, each time I find myself in a planning mode, I walk through three specific steps. First, I focus on the objective of the event. Second, I coordinate the event activities to coincide with the time the event must be accomplished, and, third, I put solutions in place for any common problem that could interfere with the timely completion of the event."

Remember that the primary reasons recruiters ask you to discuss your weaknesses are to determine your ability to be honest and candid and to identify what you are **specifically** doing to correct your weaknesses. To communicate that you are always perfect is to be less than honest and will cause a recruiter to determine that you are unqualified for the position.

When you discuss your weaknesses, be careful that you do not preface your remarks by saying, "One of my weaknesses...." Applicants do this frequently. When it occurs, a recruiter is forced to examine the **other** weaknesses that are inferred by this statement. The amount of time in the interview that you have to emphasize your achievements is then limited because the recruiter is focusing on a discussion of your weaknesses.

Preparing To Discuss Failure

It is critically important that you go into any interview prepared to discuss a failure. Remember that a failure is simply the nonaccomplishment of an objective. It isn't necessarily earth-shattering. It won't necessarily wind up on the front page of *USA Today*.

"Roger, I got caught off guard," an applicant sometimes says to me. "They asked me for a failure. I couldn't come up with one." **Don't let this happen to you.** There are two key factors that are important about communicating a failure to a company:

1) Companies want to see that you have enough self-confidence to be honest and forthright in describing a failure.

2) They also want to know what you **learned specifically** from the failure and what **broad** application this has for your future.

Companies will determine that if you have never failed, you've probably set your objectives too low. Before hiring, companies want to know how an applicant **reacted** to an adverse situation. A top recruiter once told me, "I want to see someone who has crashed into a brick wall. I want to know how they've reacted — if they've **learned** from the failure. Please don't bring me anyone who hasn't failed." I absolutely agree, so be prepared to discuss a failure. And, don't be talked out of it. Once you've given a failure, accept responsibility for it, even if the failure was due to a subordinate who worked for you. **Nothing is worse than attempting to justify the failure.**

The best example of failure you can give is one for which you were solely responsible. It came from your lack of performance, efficient time management, organizational planning, prioritizing, or overall effective management. Remember, quality people do not justify failure — they learn from it.

When you discuss a failure with a recruiter, explain **why** you failed, how you **reacted,** and what you specifically **learned.** What you learn must have broad applicability in the future. State how the failure encouraged you to improve skills in planning, organizing, communicating, analyzing, delegating, etc. A recruiter wants to know that you can take an adverse situation and analyze how you would improve, with or without a manager to tell you what to do. Recently, an applicant told me that what she learned from a failure was that the next time she purchased specific component parts for her computer department, she would be sure to check with her boss to determine her pricing latitude. While it may have been the policy for her to check with her supervisor, she also could have analyzed her skills more thoroughly. She might have determined that she needed to be more detail-oriented or that she needed to improve her planning skills. The latter analysis is much more broad-based and can have a continuous impact on her career.

What Do You Do When Confronted With Failure?
This is a question often used to reject applicants. I encourage you to look hard at this question. It is one that is similar to being handed a stick of dynamite with a one-inch lit fuse. Be careful of it. Most people fail to note the key word, **confronted**. Here is the normal response I hear: "Well, the first thing I would do is analyze why I failed." We say, "But you haven't failed." What you've just told the company is, "The first thing I would do is proceed to fail, and then analyze why."

Let's look at this situation for a moment. I tell you, "You're coming to my hotel to interview with me. The road that you normally travel is blocked because it is being torn up to put in a new sewer system. What would you do?" You might say, "Well, I can't go down the road, so I'll turn around and go back home." I doubt that is what you would do. I think you would find an alternate route. If I pointed that out, you would say, "Of course that's what I would do." Yet, when I asked you what you would do, you talked about the failure.

The best answer I ever received to this question came from an applicant from North Carolina. I'll never forget it. She looked at me and, using hand gestures, said, "I can tell you one thing, Mr. Cameron, I wouldn't fail. If I can't get up the hill one way (she used her left hand to point), then I'll come up the other way (using her right hand to point in a different direction)." I don't care what the specific words were — her answer was beautiful. She wasn't going to allow circumstances to make her fail.

A good friend of mine who recruits for Procter & Gamble said, "Roger, please bring me people who can **make things happen**. I don't want you recommending people to me who throw up their hands and accept the failure the minute the going gets tough. That is not what we're looking for. We want people who can work through difficult situations and problems and accomplish their objectives."

In a recent trip to the East Coast, I asked an interviewee what he would do when confronted with failure. The individual looked at me and said, "The first thing I do when I am confronted with failure is re-analyze the objective." You can't get a worse answer than that. He said essentially that he would analyze his objective and **lower it**. If all we had to do was lower our objective every time we were confronted with failure, we would never fail.

Another frequent response is, "Well, the first thing I do when confronted with failure is let my boss know of a pending failure." My response is always the same: " God forbid you work for Roger Cameron, because it's only going to happen one time. I hire people to lay **solutions** — **not problems** — at my feet."

To read this book and simply learn answers to questions isn't what this book is all about. I expect you to analyze yourself and ask, "Am I really a make-it-happen type person? When I confront failure, do I do something about it? Do I automatically find an excuse to rationalize why it is all right to fail, or do I figure out a different solution to accomplish the objective?" If it isn't the latter, do yourself a favor and stay out of Corporate America. It is an extremely competitive environment. Those people who do not have the ability to find solutions to difficult tasks will fail.

Can you imagine a top Fortune 500 company coming to me and saying, "Roger, we would like to pay you a good fee to travel around the world and find us people who, when confronted with problems, give them to us." Wouldn't that be absurd? Quite the contrary, companies come to me and say, "Roger, bring me people who are good problem solvers." "What do you do when confronted with failure?" is a loaded question. Be prepared for it to be asked in many different ways. It won't necessarily come as obviously as I've asked it. It's the concept you must understand.

A Word About GPA

It is unrealistic to assume everyone hired by Corporate America must have a grade point average of 3.8 or 4.0. Is there anything wrong with a low GPA? Maybe. If you don't have the ability to be an outstanding performer, then, yes, there's something wrong with it.

I want you to realize that we consider a GPA to be an **indicator**. It's really not proof of anything. It's only an indication that you may be an average, above-average, or below-average performer, depending on the GPA. But the **real** proof of your abilities lies in your ability to be an outstanding bottom-line performer. Unfortunately, I've seen applicants with high GPAs who were unable to do this, and I have brought to Corporate America some absolutely outstanding people who held low GPAs. For example, one young man had a 2.0, but every one of his supervisors raved about his outstanding performance. He was consistently rated by his superiors as the best they had supervised. He was able to convert the knowledge he gained from academics to bottom-line performance. **Under no circumstances am I suggesting you be casual about a low GPA.** However, I want you to understand, as you enter Corporate America, that education is considered a **tool,** not a ticket. Without a strong GPA and without quality work experience, Corporate America may not be in your future. As the economics of supply versus demand is running against you, it will be extremely difficult, and may be impossible, for you to get through the door of most corporations. Don't try to outguess what the market will be as you graduate. Prepare for a bad market.

Never justify a low GPA. Once, when I asked an applicant about his low GPA, he said his priorities were simply in the wrong place. I said, "If you were to go back and do it over, would you do it differently?" He replied, "No, I don't feel I would." And with that, I ruled him out. **Be careful suggesting that, in retrospect, you would still achieve only poor or fair performance. Never** defend poor performance.

Handle your GPA head-on. Don't back away from it. And don't say you went to college to be "well-rounded"; therefore, your social life and extra-curricular activities necessarily detracted from the effort you put in your studies. There are many students with high GPAs who are also well-rounded. Don't explain away a low GPA. Confront it. It had to be either a question of poor judgment or a question of intellect. Let's hope it was the former.

Companies are looking for people who **learn** from their experiences and who wouldn't go back and do everything the same. For example, if you had a low GPA, you learned that the purpose of college is academics, not extracurricular activities. Square your shoulders and simply admit that you didn't accomplish what you had the capability of doing. You'd like the opportunity to go back and redo it, but that's not possible. Explain that you've had many experiences which gave proof of your potential for quality performance, and you can prove your capability now.

Asking Quality Questions

Asking quality questions during an interview is equally as important as your ability to answer questions. You will be judged on your intelligence; your comprehension of the job, the company, and the industry; your ability to express yourself; and the ability to ask a question that will get the information you're looking for. You may think that questions will come to mind when you get into an interview. I can tell you that questions don't come to you. Prepare **before** you go into the interview. This preparation should consist of developing questions related to the position you are seeking. The questions must be specific to that company, position, and career path.

If your questions are about benefits, locations, promotions, and other irrelevant factors, you'll risk being eliminated. Take the position and break it down into its component parts. The breakdown could include product, customer, and bonus for a sales position and equipment, maintenance, and people for a production position. In an interview, focus on one component at a time. All the questions should relate to that component and then move on to another.

One way to develop questions is to picture yourself backing out of your driveway on your way to a corporate job. Where are you going? What will you do when you get there? With whom? With what? For how long? Focus on the details of the position.

Corporations produce and make available to the general public various types of corporate literature such as annual reports, company overviews, and newsletters. Be sure to ask for this literature. It is an excellent source of information from which you can formulate questions. An efficient way to develop questions is to write them down as you read the literature. If you don't, you may overlook something and ask a question that has been answered in the literature. This may give the recruiter the impression that you don't have the professional courtesy to read their literature, which is a definite "no-no" when most company brochures are produced by the thousands and cost $5 to $7 each.

One of the techniques to use in developing questions that are company specific is to use the name of the company or the company's product line in the questions. The questions will have the appearance of being asked specifically for that company. For example, a question like, "What is your turnover rate?" can be strengthened if you say instead, "Obviously, at Mobil Oil, which is a quality company in the top 10 largest companies in America, you're very concerned about turnover," or "At Mobil, what is the tenure of your labor force?" Now, you have made the question very specific to Mobil.

Be aware that asking certain questions has pitfalls. For example, companies are very sensitive about their new products. Don't ask questions such as, "What new products are you bringing to the market?" This normally is a very secret process and not one that would be openly discussed. The question would show your naiveté. Use good judgment in asking questions which might include using qualifiers. For example, you might **reword** the question by saying, "Is there any new product you are bringing to the marketplace that you can discuss at this time?"

Each of your questions should be worded so that a recruiter can answer it in a few minutes. You might find the words, "one or two" useful in forming your question. "Could you tell me the two most frequent reasons for maintenance breakdown in your production line?" "Can you tell me the two most frequent reasons for turnover with your personnel?" You don't need to know all the reasons why people quit or why machinery breaks down — just one or two of the most important ones. Therefore, you may find this technique beneficial in asking quality questions. Most important, it will save **your** interviewing time.

Many applicants are careless about giving away too much of their time in our interviews by asking poor questions. Here is a good example: "Could you tell me about the typical day in the life of the person holding this job position?" If you ask this question, the recruiter will have to take at least 10-15 minutes of your 30-45 minute interview to reply. While it may be enlightening to you, it won't accomplish the objective of the interview, which is for the company to find out enough about you to invite you to a follow-up. You will get the answer to this question in follow-up interviews. Realize that poor questions in an initial interview could be great ones during the follow-up process.

Sometimes a recruiter will use most of the interview time and then ask you if you have any questions. **Be careful**. If you say no because you think the time is up, you'll be sending out a negative signal. On the other hand, if you say **yes** you do have questions, the recruiter may not pursue you because of the lack of time to answer your questions. A better way of handling it would be to say, "Yes, I have more questions but none that I need answers to at this time. I can already tell you, I have a very strong interest in your company, and I'll save my questions to be answered in my follow-up interview." **Be careful**. Make this statement **only** if you're out of time. And, **never** make this statement of interest if it is not there.

I have also known recruiters who brought in applicants, sat them down, and stated, "Of course, you must have a thousand questions. Why don't you ask and I'll answer." This happens frequently, and you **must** be prepared for it.

I hope I've made my point. You must be serious about doing your homework and being prepared to ask quality questions. It's difficult to get hired when you don't show intelligence, curiosity, and comprehension.

Asking Negative Questions

Consider how you will ask questions that address issues that may not be positive selling points for a company — issues such as turnover rate, safety programs, quality of products, delivery of products. Your questions must be asked in a way that does not suggest you are a cynical person.

For example, instead of saying, "What percentage of your products are returned because of poor manufacturing quality?" consider saying, "I'm sure your company mandates quality product manufacturing. Can you give me some insight into the percentage of product that is returned?" When asking about the company's safety record, instead of asking, "Could you tell me about your safety program?" I recommend saying, "A company with your quality standards is obviously very concerned about its safety program. I'd like to hear about your safety record." Again, the key is to make the tone of your question positive.

Another negative connotation is made when you use the word "type" as in "With what type of people will I work?" Avoid the use of this word. Articulate your questions more precisely.

Colloquialisms And Qualifiers

College students are strong competitors for the gold medal in using qualifiers in their conversations that indicate they are unsure of themselves or that they are indecisive — words such as "I think," "I believe," or "probably." What you say to the recruiter when you use these qualifiers is, "I'm not really sure, but here's what my guess would be." In an interview, we're not asking for your guess; we're asking for the way it **is**. Even worse, you are suggesting you don't want to be held responsible for your statement.

I remember I had a young recruiter working for me at one time who had difficulty expressing himself in a positive, confident manner. For instance, when I asked him what time it was, he would look at his watch and say, "I **think** it's **about** . . ." instead of saying, "It's 1:09." Recognize the importance of eliminating qualifiers like this from your conversation before you interview.

Colloquialisms are fine in informal conversation but not in an interview. Do not use words, such as "yeah," "roger," or "check" for "yes." And, if you have developed the habit of using "you know" in conversation, work hard to erase it completely. I quickly remind applicants that if "we knew," we wouldn't be asking the question. There is no reason for you to ever use the phrase, "you know."

I remember one individual who began and ended every sentence with "okay." This is not something you can do and call yourself a good communicator. Be very careful of colloquial expressions and qualifiers. **Listen** to your tape recorder. It won't lie to you!

Involving Spouses
If you are married, should your spouse be involved in your career choices? Absolutely. This is one of the most important moves you're going to make in your lifetime.

Examine this critical move as a team. Invite your spouse to read this book so he or she can be constructively critical of your answers when you prepare for your interviews.

Spouses, be very honest in your critiques. This is not the time to be nice or let things slide. If you do, your spouse will have a tendency to make the same mistakes in the interview that were made during preparation. While it is frustrating for applicants, spouses' critiques must include telling them every time a word is misused, pointing out when they ramble, indicating when they imply but don't state, and informing them when they say, "you know." Ask yourself if you understand exactly what your spouse is saying. Does your spouse come to the point immediately, answer the entire question with substance, and have an enthusiastic voice? Will your spouse excite the listener? Detach yourself. Be a strict evaluator. You must be very demanding of a quality performance. It is the only way to help your spouse improve.

Use a tape recorder. You and your spouse can better evaluate what you say when you listen to a recording. The tape recorder will play back exactly what you've said and won't lie to you. What you give it is what it will give back to you.

Camcorders are very popular. They are becoming less expensive to purchase and can be beneficial to use in your preparation. (You may want to consider borrowing one.) They provide an excellent way to determine if your posture and facial expression are natural, if you maintain good eye contact, whether you smile, and basically if your "second" appearance represents you as you want to be represented. I strongly recommend that you dress for the videotape as you would for your interviews. By dressing properly, you will be in the proper frame of mind. I **do not** recommend using the camera to grade your answers, verbal enthusiasm, voice inflection, diction, articulation, and conciseness. I have found that you have a tendency to automatically watch yourself but **not** listen to yourself. The bottom line is that both the tape recorder and camcorder have a place in helping you prepare.

Working With Other Students

Find other students who have the same outstanding qualities as yourself and work together to prepare. Arrange an evening once a week when you can all get together to share questions and ideas and to critique each other. As you work with others, make a pact that you're going to be honest in critiquing one another. Be willing to provide ideas. Be adventurous in responding to questions. There are many ways to prepare. If you'll work with other students, it will force you to prepare. While you may not want to embarrass yourself in front of others, those embarrassments and frustrations will cost you nothing. Where it will cost you is in front of a company.

Researching Companies

I'm frequently asked about the importance of researching companies before interviewing with them. Let me stress that the first priority is what you know about yourself — your background, skills, and interests. Unfortunately, many applicants spend more time researching companies. Balance the amount of time you spend preparing to articulate your skills and accomplishments with learning about the company. Doing this will prepare you to make the important connections for the recruiter between your background, skills and interests, and company objectives. You will also be more capable of asking questions that are relevant.

I have had many more applicants ruled out in corporate interviews for what they did not know about themselves than for what they did not know about the company. Earlier in this chapter, I suggested getting company literature and taking notes as you read it. Highlighters are valuable tools for this exercise, as are 3x5 cards for writing questions. In addition to reading company literature, attempt to find people who work for the company and are willing to discuss the company with you. The information you get from these individuals may be better than all the literature you could read.

Recruiters have said to me, "Your applicants are extremely well prepared." This is true because applicants I recommend to companies recognize the interview is one of the most important steps they will take in life. My applicants are proactive. They get their hands on every book they can. They talk with every recruiter they can. They learn the best way to have successful interviews.

If at any time in an interview a recruiter suggests that you might be using someone else's answers, stop him immediately. Let him know you have worked hard to be prepared but that you are not using other people's answers. Explain that you have read interviewing handbooks — Roger Cameron's or any other author's handbook — and explain that you have practiced by tape recording your replies.

Let the recruiter know the amount of work you've put in before interviewing.

Appendix A provides additional information on definitions and critical characteristics for interview preparation.

Taking Time For Personal Development

If your career is important to you, take the time to read the periodicals and books that will enhance your professional growth. Recruiters want people with curiosity and a strong desire to learn and grow. Your only way of growing **with** Corporate America and remaining knowledgeable and competitive is to read. I suggest you either read or relegate yourself to going through life being a follower versus a leader.

Television gives you very limited information. Don't rely on it. Don't accept that you are too busy to read. Pick up a book for 30 minutes before going to bed at night. Take a book with you for the weekend to read on an airplane or in a car. Find the time necessary for this development activity — no matter what. I can't imagine anyone being serious about success who doesn't read four to six books per month — at the minimum.

An applicant once told me he didn't like to read and didn't intend to. I asked him how he saw himself gaining the necessary knowledge to be an effective manager in Corporate America. He looked confused and responded that he had already gained the necessary knowledge with a baccalaureate degree. His response revealed his naiveté about the necessity of a continuous personal development program to prepare for the rigors of the business world.

Appendix B lists books, periodicals, seminars, and tapes I recommend for your personal development to help you prepare for corporate interviews.

**THE SECRET OF SUCCESS IS DOING
WHAT YOU OUGHT TO DO,
WHEN YOU OUGHT TO DO IT,
WHETHER YOU WANT TO OR NOT,
NO DEBATE.**
— **Walter Hailey, Jr.**

CHAPTER 5

"A must graduation gift for any high school senior. An excellent basic book about the real world of work. I believe that the information in this book should be turned into a required course for all high school students."

—Paula Brown
Board of Trustees
Bruceville-Eddy ISD

CHAPTER 5

Consider The Physical Factors Of Interviewing

Being On Time

Few behaviors can hinder your climb to the top of the corporate ladder more than being late when you make commitments. When you are late in arriving for an event or appointment, in accomplishing an objective, in turning in a report, or in sending a thank-you note, the impression you leave is less than satisfactory. **Make it a habit — never be late.**

I encourage you to look at being late for an interview from the point of view of a recruiter. When you are late by even a minute, the recruiter is placed in the uncomfortable position of wondering where you are. Numerous possibilities present themselves — perhaps you are in the elevator, maybe you have forgotten the appointment, or perhaps you've even had an accident. In any case, you know where you are and how late you are going to be, but the recruiter knows nothing other than the fact that you are not there! As the minutes go by, the recruiter doesn't know whether to wait, make a phone call, or leave to do other work. Your action has resulted in the recruiter wasting time. After you force a recruiter's anxiety level to climb, it may be difficult for you to get an objective interview.

The message is: Consider what being late says about you — **nothing good!**

Clothes And Appearance

Once you start to work for a company, you'll be measured primarily according to your performance. When you interview, you're going to be judged on every possible factor, including what you wear. It's sad to hear of someone who has worked hard to secure a good education, spent money to build a resume, put in time preparing for interviews, and is ruled out because of the way he or she is dressed.

If you're outstanding and have done everything right, it's possible but doubtful your clothes will rule you out of a job — unless they are unprofessional. But if the recruiter feels something about you is questionable and that is compounded by a poor appearance, then your clothes will become a major factor. I recommend that you read John Molloy's *Dress For Success* (for men or women). Acceptable business attire for men has been established and widely practiced for many years. On the other hand, business attire for women is not universally understood, and women can easily make serious mistakes when they take advice from well-meaning people (even clothing store personnel) who do not understand what constitutes professional business clothing for women. Therefore, it is very important for women to read Mr. Molloy's *Dress For Success For Women*. The best rule of thumb for men and women to remember regarding appearances in the entire interviewing and hiring process is this:

> Your physical appearance should imply that you are professional and competent and that you can get the job done. This does not mean you should look dull, but if you err, it should be on the side of being conservative versus highly fashionable. Remember, you are not trying to please your friends or the fashion experts but rather the people who make hiring decisions. These individuals are usually older and conservative (at least in their business appearance), and care more about what you can accomplish than how good-looking you are.

I recommend that women applicants have two suits for interviewing purposes. Each should have matching jacket and skirt, be made in a traditional style, and be in solid colors of either navy blue or gray.

Some national brands we recommend are Austin Reed, Cricketeer, and Jones of New York. Many styles and colors are available in women's business suits today, and you must select suits of traditional cuts and colors for interviewing. Women should not wear pin stripe suits or men's ties or try to look like men. The length of the skirt should be just below the knee to two inches below the knee. White or off-white tailored blouses are best. They should not be sheer, overly lacy, or made of a fabric commonly worn in social situations. The neckline should be discreet and professional appearing.

Shoes should be low-heeled (two inches or less is a good rule of thumb) with closed toes and heels. You should be able to stand easily and walk briskly in your shoes. Black, navy, or other dark neutral colors are best. Wear natural-colored hose with no seams or texture.

A woman's handbag should be of small or moderate size and only large enough to carry essentials. It should be what I call "a business purse" that simply gets the job done. Again, black, navy, or dark neutral colors are best.

These points are also important for women: Keep your jewelry to a minimum for an interview. One ring on each hand (at the most) and a strand of pearls or a simple gold chain is sufficient jewelry. If you wear earrings, they should be small or fit close to the earlobe. Dangling earrings are not appropriate.

Women should have a hairstyle that is neat and professional. If your hair is below shoulder length, wear it pulled back — in a chignon, French braid, or pony tail. A very tailored hairstyle is best.

Your make-up should be light. Wear shadow, blush, and lipstick that are natural-looking rather than bright or dramatic. Avoid heavy eyeliners. Your fingernails should be medium to short in length. If you wear nail polish, be sure it is clear. Keep perfume light or wear none at all.

For both men and women, the rule is to look conservative, professional, and classic. Everything should be done in moderation. That's why overdoing perfume or after-shave lotion can leave a reminder of you long after you're gone — and **not** in a positive way.

I have no idea why anyone would come to an interview wearing an alarm clock — whether it's a Big Ben you put up on the recruiter's desk or a wristwatch you wear on your arm. If I'm in the middle of an interview with an applicant and his or her alarm clock goes off, it is very disrupting. I consider it to be very unprofessional. If you need a watch that tells you every time the hour or the half-hour strikes, that's just fine, but turn it off or get rid of it before you come to an interview.

While a recruiter for a major national company was interviewing an applicant, the applicant's wristwatch went off. The recruiter got up from behind his desk and said, "Obviously, you have something more important than this interview," walked the young man to the door, and let him out. I don't blame him. It's highly inconsiderate to take an alarm clock with you to an interview.

In stressing very light jewelry for all male applicants, I suggest nothing more than a class ring, a wedding band, and a business-style wristwatch.

Men's hair should be cut in a conservative, professional style. If you have partible hair, then part it. If your hair is very fine and has a tendency to blow out of shape with the slightest breeze, then use hair spray to hold it in place. And watch out for the strange things a hat or cap can do to your hair. When you remove the hat or cap, be sure your hair is combed and well-groomed.

Men should also have two suits. Each should be two-piece and single-breasted with one and one half-inch cuffs on the pants. One suit should be navy blue and the other dark gray with a subtle, single, three-fourths inch gapped, white pin stripe. The stripe should be very discreet and only visible when you are within arms length.

It's critical that you buy two suits for your job search. Then, you won't get stuck in a situation that often can occur — when the company representative with whom you are interviewing meets you at the end of your flight and you both go to dinner. You must wear the suit you wore while traveling. That means the next day this suit will not be acceptable in appearance for your interview. You **must** have the second suit.

Your suits don't need to be extremely expensive, but they should be of good quality. There are several good brands, but one we consistently recommend is Hart, Schaffner & Marx. This company sells good quality, inexpensive business suits and knows exactly what you need in a business cut. Sometimes you can find two suits on sale for the price of one that are acceptable for interviews. Your suits should always be extremely well-pressed for interviews.

Your shirts should be white with button-down collars. I usually suggest 100 percent cotton. Many business people who are constantly on the road have to send out their shirts to hotel laundries. Let me assure you that if you travel the circuit I travel, you won't be able to wear 99 percent of the shirts returned from these laundries. One side of the collar goes one way, the other another way. That's why you should wear shirts with button-down collars. Don't assume that the shirts you send to the laundry will be ironed satisfactorily. A typical scenario is that you get your laundry back at 7:00 p.m. Your interview is at 7:00 a.m. the next morning. You wear the shirt the way it is — or you don't wear it. You have no choice. The button-down design overcomes any collar problem caused by a laundry.

Your ties should be "power ties" — bold in color — so that they are the focal point. There's a very simple reason for this. When you travel, you can't take four or five suits with you and change your suit frequently. If you want to switch your tie in the middle of the day, 90 percent of those around you will think you've changed your entire suit.

You can't buy a $15 tie today that's acceptable for an interview. You will need to spend about $30 or more. Don't ruin an interview for the sake of saving $10 or $15.

Wear good-quality socks that are over-the-calf, such as socks from Brooks Brothers. You can run in these socks, and they will stay up. Don't wear socks that bunch down around your ankles, as I so often see in interviews.

The shoe I recommend is a wine-colored, wing-tipped cordovan with a tassel. When you travel you can't carry a lot of different shoes. You can wear the shoe I recommend with a tan, brown, black, or blue suit. It's an extremely acceptable shoe and is a good choice for interviews and casual wear. Be sure your shoes are well-shined. There is no excuse for any other appearance. There are even small shoeshine kits available that you can carry in your pocket.

Occasionally, a recruiter will tell you to wear casual clothes for dinner or hiring sessions other than the actual interview sessions. But what does that mean? There is no official definition of casual clothes. For men I recommend quality slacks, a shirt, a tie, and a sport jacket. (A suit jacket worn with slacks is **not** a sport jacket.) For women I recommend a skirt and blouse with a blazer or a dress — not pants.

If you are a man and find your dinner companion isn't wearing a tie or a jacket, it's very simple to remove yours. It's easy to dress down, but impossible to dress up. Let me assure you that if you are in an interview and you're under-dressed, you can't make up the difference there. Know ahead of time what will be expected of you. If you are not advised by the company with which you are interviewing, ask what is appropriate.

Remember, what you wear when you go to work for a company will be at your own discretion within their professional set of standards. You'll be measured primarily on your work performance, but in the job search, your clothes are a key factor that companies use to evaluate your judgment.

Glasses

Sunglasses should never be worn in an interview. Recruiters want to see your expression and have eye contact with you. It is very difficult, if not impossible, to see through tinted glasses. Some of you wear the photogrey glasses that change with sunlight. The unfortunate thing is that, many times, when you come into a hotel or into the placement office to interview, you will sit next to a window. Photogrey will automatically tint the glass. These glasses are perfectly all right to work in under certain circumstances, but they are not the best for interviewing.

I also recommend that when you purchase glasses you choose professional frames that will be appropriate with the clothes you wear to your interviews. The easiest way to be sure your selection is a good one is to wear one of your interview suits and try on the frames in front of a full-length mirror.

Most importantly, have your glasses fitted professionally so that you won't have to push your glasses into place repeatedly during the interview. Applicants often have developed such a habit of doing this that they make the motion of pushing their glasses into place even when they are not wearing them. Most optometrists will adjust your glasses free of charge while you wait. Therefore, take advantage of this service and make sure your glasses fit properly.

Posture

Often, the chairs in which you will sit while interviewing contribute to poor posture. Sometimes you can't help but put your elbows on the arm rests because of the way they are positioned. When you do, your hands are up in your face. I've seen applicants talk through their hands or lean on them as if they were tired.

Posture is important. Sit up straight in the chair. **Control** your environment — don't let the environment control **you**. You can change your posture. Don't sit stiffly. Be natural, but with good posture. And feel free to cross your legs if that is a comfortable position for you.

Don't sit on the front edge of a chair or couch. Sit **back** in the chair. When you want to emphasize a point, you can then lean forward and stress that point. If you sit on the edge of your chair and lean forward, you may fall off. I've actually had this happen to applicants. It's embarrassing for both of us. Recruiters look for **professional** enthusiasm, not **nervous** enthusiasm. The first you can be comfortable with. But the second makes even the recruiter nervous. We like high energy, but we don't want it to drive us out of the room.

Eating

Using good manners and good judgment while you eat is also an important factor in the interviewing environment. I've seen too many applicants lose an offer because of what they did at dinner. Always finish your meal. Not eating suggests you are too nervous and lack poise and self-confidence.

The company will be paying, so be aware of the cost of what you order. Don't select the most expensive entree on the menu. That suggests that you don't understand expenses. Today, companies can't always write off all these expenses on meals.

When you order, be aware that foods with sauces can be difficult to eat without spotting your clothes. The primary purpose of the meal is to interview rather than eat. Therefore, order foods that are easy to handle — thereby reducing the risk of unsightly spills.

You may think it won't happen to you, but I've seen it happen to the very best applicants. It's very embarrassing to have a spot on your tie, shirt or pants, blouse or skirt, for the balance of an interview — especially if the spilling happened at breakfast. Getting yourself into that kind of situation suggests you aren't controlling your environment. You're losing sight of the meal's objective — which is to provide an opportunity to interview.

For dinner I suggest ordering a sauteed fish entree. Fish is easy to get into the mouth and dissolves quickly. I've watched applicants tackle entrees they must chew repeatedly. A lot of chewing doesn't allow you the crucial time to answer and ask questions.

Also, remember your manners. Since we live in such a fast-paced world, rules of etiquette are often never learned. However, business is often conducted over meals and having good manners could be very important to you. Here are some of the major tips:
• Don't start eating before your host or hostess begins.
• Cut your food up as you eat it — not all at once.
• Use your napkin.
• Don't eat while you are talking.
• Chew with your mouth closed.
• Place the napkin on your lap with the crease toward you. Never tuck it in your belt or collar.
• Remember the rule of thumb: "Solids on the left; liquids on the right." This may help you avoid using someone else's water glass instead of your own.

- Don't serve yourself items such as salt, pepper, sugar, and salad dressing before you offer it to someone else.
- Don't salt your food before you taste it. It is a signal that you are a person who makes rash decisions.
- Spoon soup away from you and sip it from the side of the spoon — without slurping.
- Remove olive pits, bones, etc. from your mouth discreetly.

Drinking

I feel there is absolutely no excuse for drinking alcohol during an interview — period. If you normally drink and are offered a drink, you may say, "I do drink on occasion, but I prefer not to while I'm interviewing." Any recruiter who doesn't accept that as professional behavior is probably with a company you wouldn't want to be with anyway.

Again, there can be no reason for drinking alcohol in an interview, and, as far as I'm concerned, the recruiter shouldn't be drinking either.

Chewing Gum

If you chew gum in an interview, expect not to be considered for the position. It is disappointing to see an applicant in an interview, at an information meeting, or at a conference attempting to communicate while chewing gum. It's rude, unprofessional, and uncalled for. When I've ruled out applicants for this reason and explained why, they were quick to tell me they would never chew gum in front of a company. Neither you nor they should be selectively unprofessional! Please, never have anything in your mouth as you talk to others.

Smoking

Here's the rule on smoking — **never** smoke during an interview. Never. If you smoke, then smoke before you go to your breakfast, lunch, or dinner meeting, but do not smoke during an interview.

When you're hired, it might be acceptable to smoke on the job or at least in designated smoking areas. However, more and more companies are hiring nonsmokers.

An alumnus of mine, who is now recruiting for an outstanding corporation, suggested to me that "smoking is the prejudice of the '90s. There is only one message here and that is to quit. When I know an interviewee is a smoker, I feel one or more of three things must be true: 1) the person doesn't care about his health or appearance, 2) the person doesn't have the discipline to quit, or 3) the person is ignorant of modern medical facts."

Foul Language

There can **never** be an excuse to use foul language in an interview, or for that matter, anyplace in Corporate America. What you're saying is that you do not have the ability to express your point of view without it. I see absolutely no excuse for foul language and always feel sorry for a person who has to communicate in that way. Do yourself a favor and never bring foul language to an interview.

Overspending

Be alert. Know what amounts you are billing to the company paying for your interview expenses. Don't be like the young man who traveled to Chicago to interview and found he didn't have the $30 cash to pay taxi fare from the airport to the client's office. All he had was credit cards, so he ordered a limousine for $120. You may say, "That was good judgment. He got himself to the company's office." But, let me assure you it was **poor** judgment to have the vice president of personnel see him pull up in a limousine billed to the expense account. This applicant did **not** get an offer. The poor judgment started when the applicant didn't take a sufficient amount of cash with him for incidental costs. It is logical that you will have to take taxis. Today, to travel on follow-up interviews without $75 or $80, or even more, in your pocket could be poor judgment.

A company is **always** measuring your judgment. From the time you leave your door, you're spending the company's money. You're going to be examined every step of the way. That applies to everything — flights, taxis, hotels, and dinners with company recruiters.

Casual Interviewing

Companies often like to see applicants in a casual setting. By having the opportunity to talk with you outside the corporate environment, recruiters feel they will be able to assess certain strengths and weaknesses more accurately.

Don't let anyone throw you off by saying, "Don't worry. Tonight is just a casual evening. We're going to chat. We'll be evaluating tomorrow during the interviews." Don't believe that for a second. Companies will try to get you off guard, and there is never any excuse for allowing this to happen. While you are with company representatives, you are always being evaluated. Don't be like the young man who exclaimed, "Oh, great!" and immediately took off his tie and shoes. That's really getting casual!

Nervous Habits

You should be able to come into an interview, regardless of the environment, and concentrate specifically on what you are doing. Interviews can take place in almost every location possible — bathrooms, hallways, parking lots, hotel rooms, or on a walk around the block. In these locations, there are many opportunities for distractions and for you to be nervous.

Control the interviewing environment. Don't let nervous habits unconsciously make you look bad. For example, in some hotels the room where the interview takes place has a window that looks out on the swimming pool. I've had applicants indicate they're more interested in checking out what's happening pool-side than they are in focusing on the interview.

Be aware that some recruiters may purposely try to distract you. They may turn on the TV, without sound, to see if you can still focus on the interview rather than the TV screen. Their actions are justifiable. They are testing you to determine whether you are easily distracted from your objective — in this case, the interview. If you don't have the ability to go into an environment and focus on the reason for being there, you won't accomplish your objective.

Many interviewees insist on fiddling with flick pens. Doing this reveals an unconscious nervous habit to the recruiter. If you are prone to this habit, make it easy on yourself and use a different kind of pen in the interview. Hold the pen only when you are actually writing with it.

Another nervous habit is swinging one leg back and forth when one leg is crossed over the other. I interviewed an applicant who did this constantly, so I suddenly took my left arm and began waving it back and forth, from my shoulder out. I continued to ask questions. The applicant stared at me. I asked, "Am I bothering you?" He said, "Yes, you really are." I then pointed out his nervous habit which had been distracting me. This may seem like a harsh response, but I wanted to emphasize this important point. He now was conscious of a subconscious nervous habit. You may say, "I would never do that." But I have seen many people with nervous habits who were not even conscious of them until I brought them to their attention. If you have this tendency, sit with both feet on the floor during the interview so that you avoid distracting or irritating the recruiter.

Sometimes, I want to say to applicants, "Would you mind **sitting** on your hands?" Almost every moment they're attempting to communicate with their hands. The gestures are so distracting that it is difficult to concentrate on what is being said. It's okay to gesture on occasion, but in the interview you should do everything in moderation. Talking with your hands becomes annoying. The recruiters may try to imagine you at a staff meeting and may feel your habit is too irritating to consider you for the position.

Many hotels or interviewing rooms have noisy window air conditioning units, but sometimes applicants will ignore the noise. They'll still talk in a normal tone of voice instead of lifting their voices to overcome the air conditioning. If I have to turn off the a.c. in order to hear applicants, I'm going to reject them. If they are not aware enough to raise their voice over the noise, then they're really not the kind of people my companies are paying me to find.

Also, there's the problem of what some people do with their rings. I've had applicants take off a wedding band and try it on each finger, not even aware of what they're doing. One man got the ring stuck on his thumb and had a hard time getting it off. Another put both little fingers in the wedding band. They got stuck, and I literally had to hold the wedding band in place, so this individual could pull his fingers out.

When a ring falls to the floor, it invariably rolls under the bed, under the couch, or under the table. It's embarrassing. You're sitting there in your good-looking two-piece suit. Then, suddenly, you're on the floor, trying to retrieve a ring from under the bed.

Make a concerted effort to be aware of any habits you have which may be objectionable to others. Either eliminate them or at least develop a strategy for making it impossible to use them in an interview.

What To Take To An Interview
When you go to an interview, take with you a pen and a spiral notebook that is **small** enough to fit into your suit coat pocket. Make sure your pen is noise-proof and has no parts that click when you hold it. You will use the notebook to record addresses and phone

numbers if recruiters and companies want you to call or send them something. You should pull out your notebook when you are introduced to someone and write down the individual's name. I know how frequently you are introduced, and this helps you remember names.

If the individual is wearing a name tag, that is different. You can look at the name tag and have it remind you. Otherwise, do not be embarrassed about writing down the individual's name — particularly if you are in an interview where there are several recruiters. It's critical to write down a person's name so that you can send a thank-you letter later. Do not be reluctant to ask an individual how to spell his or her name for clarification, "Tim? Or, did you say Jim?" There is absolutely nothing wrong with that. I know of many embarrassing situations when people have forgotten names.

The small notebook you use in the interview should be clean so you don't have to thumb through to find a page on which to make a note on. When you're finished making notes on a particular company, tear the sheet out of the notebook and put the notebook into your coat pocket. As you go into your next interview, you can again be prepared to write on a clean page.

CHAPTER 6

"The author draws on his wealth of experience from the interviewer side of the desk to offer extremely valuable information for candidates. If you follow the advice in this comprehensive, career planning and job search book, many career doors will open for you."

—Frank G. Carney, Director
Career Planning and Placement
Louisiana State University

CHAPTER 6

Understand Interviewing Techniques

Time To Verbalize

Students have a phenomenon in their backgrounds called "moving to the next step based on the observation of past performance." You go to elementary school, are observed by your teachers, and are graded. Based upon those grades, you take the next step by moving on to middle school. Based on observation and grades, you go on to high school. The procedure follows you into college. You are observed and graded. However, when you leave college and make the decision to go into business, you must **verbalize** your past successes. You're not afforded the opportunity to be **observed** before being hired. Whether you are hired is based on how you verbalize success in the interview. Many students are not prepared to verbalize past accomplishments or to tell about themselves in a logical sequence. They haven't practiced doing so. This is absolutely a critical point: Verbalize your accomplishments and record them into a tape recorder. I can assure you that whatever you **give** that tape recorder, it will give you **back**. When you listen to the recording, be honest. Ask yourself the following questions: Did I communicate in an articulate fashion? Was I concise? Did I say what I wanted to say without rambling? Did I address the question directly? Did I accentuate my competencies? It is unfortunate that many students who have been good academic performers in the past do not have the ability to verbalize their performances. Therefore, they have been ruled out by industry for positions as development candidates.

No company will come out and observe you in college or at your work environment (for example, for a period of five months), then, if they like what they see, give you an offer. You have to describe your skills, experiences, and successes in a series of interviews. In this section, I will give you some ideas about how to be successful in the interview.

Evading A Question

Never evade a question. When a recruiter asks a specific question, answer it. Listen carefully to the question and be certain you understand it so that you do not appear to evade it. For example, if the question is, "What is your location preference?" don't reply that you are open, but rather give a preference which is regional, such as the Southeast or the Northwest. State it in the broadest of terms — for example, "east of the Mississippi River."

A question that calls for a "yes" or "no" should **immediately** be answered with the words "yes" or "no," and then you may support it. Too often, when I ask a particular question, the applicant replies with a lot of rhetoric, and I must sit there and wonder if this is going to lead to a "yes" or a "no." Have the self-confidence to say "yes" or "no" immediately and then support your answer. When that individual sitting in front of me says "yes" and then supports it, I know exactly where we're going. I don't have to question or wonder. I don't have to remember all the rhetoric to determine the answer.

Spontaneous And Reflective Questions

You will be asked two types of questions in an interview: spontaneous and reflective. **Spontaneous** questions take about five percent of any interview. Examples include the following: How do you pronounce your last name? Where did you go to college? What was your grade point average? What was your major? Where is your home town? Obviously, these answers are on the tip of your tongue, and you can quickly, spontaneously answer them.

The most frequently asked question is the **reflective** question. You must cover these four basic steps in responding:

1) **Listen.** Actively listen to each word the interviewer puts into a sentence.
2) **Reflect.** Think about the question. How will you answer?
3) **Organize** the answer in your mind.
4) **Deliver** your answer.

I might add a fifth step — knowing when to **"shut up."** Too many people continue to talk when, in fact, they have already given the answer.

Not listening is the number one reason applicants are eliminated from an interview. Listening comes before anything else in an interview. You must understand exactly what the recruiter is asking and then address the question directly. As the recruiter asks you a question, give an indication with a nod of your head or movement of your eyes that you are listening. Let the recruiter know you are eagerly listening to everything. Also, be sure you don't attempt to show signs of wanting to answer the question before the recruiter is finished. That is very poor manners. You should never answer a question until you have heard the complete question. Some applicants make me feel I actually need to stop asking the question because in some magical way they have been able to read my mind. I know they haven't, but they make me feel that way. Listen intently. Show signs of listening. Do not attempt to respond before the recruiter is finished.

When you are asked a **reflective** question, it's perfectly all right for you to take three, four, or even five seconds to think. This is much better than restating the question. Please don't do that. Ordinarily, this suggests that the recruiter lacked the ability to articulate. The reason you restate the question is just because you want two or three seconds to think. It is perfectly all right to simply take a few quiet moments to reflect.

You should always be as spontaneous as you can. But, you should never be spontaneous to the point of hurting yourself. Take the time to think through your answer so that you can deliver it fluently. Avoid the danger of talking, then thinking, then ending up rambling. Recruiters will give you a lot more credit for a few seconds of silence — and then a well-delivered answer — than for being spontaneous and, therefore, inadequate with a **reflective** question.

Today, the effective use of time is becoming more and more critical as companies assign people more work to do. Industry wants to see this work done in an eight- to nine-hour day — instead of adding hours to complete the job. Corporations are not looking for workaholics. They want people who use time effectively, who work "smart," who are **peak performers.** An interviewer wants to see if you have a logical, organized mind. He wants to discover during the interview whether or not you **organize your answers.** Do you maximize the amount of interviewing that can be done in the time period?

Evaluating Your Answer
Your answer will be evaluated in three ways, regardless of who is asking the question.
- **First,** the **substance** or content of your answer.
  - Did you give a **complete** answer to a question, or did the interviewer have to ask two or three questions to get a full reply?
  - Are you able to convey a complete thought and make your point?
  - Do you find people misinterpret you?

- **Second,** the **delivery** you use. Deliver your answer so that your audience understands exactly what your point of view is.

Frequently, an interviewee will forget the question — or go off on a tangent, misusing the interview time — and give irrelevant information.

- How **expressive** is your voice?
- Are you sensitive to the impact of your voice? If you scream, do people tend to scream back? If you whisper, do they whisper back? Begin to **notice what affect your voice has on others and how effective your voice can be.**
- Do you use proper intonation, voice volume, facial expression, and **verbal enthusiasm** as you talk? Do you have the ability to get someone else to respond to your ideas or thoughts because of your enthusiasm? Do you excite?
- Can you make your point without being abrasive, combative, or abrupt?
- Do you deliver in a fluid manner?
- Do you emphasize key words?
- Do you mumble?
- Are you speaking too loudly or too softly?
- Do you drop the volume of your voice at the end of sentences?
- Do you talk too quickly?
- Do you slur your words together?
- Do you talk slower than is normal for a conversation? Are you picking your words too carefully?

- **Third**, the **conciseness** of your answers.
  - Do you give answers with as few words as possible but deliver substance? Practice "interviewing" using a tape recorder or camcorder to improve your ability to communicate your views in minimum time. Nothing will help you more with recruiters. An employee must have the ability **to accomplish maximum tasks in minimum time.**

Use the following exercises to critique your articulation and speech patterns.

Exercise #1

Prepare an answer to the request, "Tell me about yourself." This is a very common interview question. You need to represent your background to an interviewer in a clear and concise manner. An interview is a **conversation** with the interviewer. Therefore, be very careful not to come across as though you are giving a canned answer or speech. Your discussion about yourself should be sincere and natural.

Use a tape recorder to record your reply. Concentrate on speaking clearly and enunciating your words. Be aware of your voice projection and the reaction of your audience. Have another person listen to the recording and help you evaluate it using the questions for "Evaluating Your Answer" (substance, delivery, conciseness) in this chapter. If you do not use a tape recorder, ask another person to critique you after you deliver your reply.

Exercise #2

Prepare a **speech** on a subject of importance to you. Present this speech to your spouse or a friend, **and** record it on tape. The purpose of this exercise is to reveal to you how your speaking pattern varies when you give a speech versus when you carry on a conversation. In an interview, it is very important for you to be conversational, natural, and sincere — you should NOT sound like you are giving a speech. Listen to the tape recording of your speech. Compare it to the tape of your reply in Exercise #1. You should notice the differences in your speaking patterns so you will not fall into "giving a speech" in an interview.

Frequent Mistakes

Over the many years corporate recruiters have interviewed my applicants, we have asked them to give us feedback on each list of applicants they interviewed and their reasons for acceptance or decline. These feedback slates have reached into the thousands and reveal the three most frequent reasons applicants are eliminated from interviews.

1) **Doesn't actively listen.** A recent study published by a major periodical (which requires strong proof and evidence for any article they print) showed that top managers in Corporate America spend 73 percent of their time listening. Therefore, if during the first 30 minutes of communication with a company you prove your lack of ability to listen, you can imagine how that influences their decision to hire you as a development candidate. Often, an applicant will listen to the overall question but fail to listen to **each word**. Thus, the answer may be incomplete. If you can't listen properly, recruiters will understandably be concerned about your skill in communicating. Applicants often think they have had a great interview when, in fact, they were not even addressing the questions asked.

2) **Doesn't excite.** Excitement generally comes from your verbal skills to communicate — your verbal enthusiasm, the inflection of your voice, how you walk, and your handshake.

3) **Rambles.** The habit of rambling implies to the recruiter that you didn't organize your answer, didn't have confidence in it, and didn't think it out. You must think and then talk, or your answer won't have substance. Too frequently, what you're doing is talking — and then thinking.

Don't ignore these three frequent mistakes. Write them on the cuff of your shirt or the palm of your hand. Don't get casual about these points. Again and again, companies cite these as the most common reasons to rule out an applicant. If you remember nothing else in this book, you will then be head-and-shoulders above most applicants interviewing coast to coast. More recruiter comments on mistakes are discussed in Chapter 8.

Frequent Reasons for Rejection
- **Doesn't actively listen**
- **Doesn't excite**
- **Rambles**

High Energy Level

Companies come to me and say, "Don't bring me applicants who are tired. We want people with **high energy**." In a corporate sense, high energy means the ability of an individual to put out as much work the eighth hour of the day as he or she does in the first hour of the day. After all, people are paid as much for the last hour as for the first hour.

In an interview, we measure high energy in three ways.

1) **Visible high energy — how you walk.** Do you demonstrate a sense of urgency? A favorite recruiter at Texas Instruments likes to stand outside his door about five minutes before the time of an interview. He watches the applicant turn the corner down the hall and observes the applicant's pace. He likes to see an applicant who has an energetic way of walking. Keep in mind that you may be observed outside the office where you are interviewed and maintain a lively pace no matter where you are.

2) **Feeling of high energy — handshake.** When you shake hands, it should be purposeful. You should step **into** the **handshake**, whether it's with a man or a woman. The handshake should be firm — full into the hand, showing a physical demonstration of high energy rather than strength. Energy should flow from **you** to the person with whom you're shaking hands.

3) **Audible high energy — enthusiasm in your voice.** Recruiters want to hear the energy in your voice. Does your voice convey

excitement and eagerness for the work with changes in its tone and pitch?

I remember listening to a professor of military science talk to an ROTC group at a major southern college. He had a strong voice and delivery. But, I noticed that he turned his audience off about five minutes into his speech. They were looking at the floor, out the windows, and at their books and papers. At first, I couldn't understand why his audience was paying so little attention to him. Then, I realized he had absolutely no voice inflection. His voice was booming, but everything came out in a monotone. He didn't **modulate** his voice.

Verbal enthusiasm and voice inflection should go hand in hand. Too often, companies say to me, "Roger, the applicant said the correct things but not in a convincing manner."

Making Things Happen

I was in Colorado Springs speaking with an individual whom I had just declined. I asked the young man if there was any insight or help I could give him. He said, "Mr. Cameron, could you tell me in one sentence what it is that recruiters are looking for most in a development candidate?" It almost made me think I had made a mistake in declining him. I replied that recruiters are simply looking for an individual who can **make things happen** — who is goal-oriented and success-driven. Corporations don't want to hire people who feel it is satisfactory to fail as long as they have an excuse. Typical excuses encountered include the following: "Oh, I'm sorry I'm late. I didn't know it was going to rain." "I didn't know Sally was going to take off for four weeks of vacation." "I didn't know the parts were going to come in late." "I didn't know my car was going to have a flat tire." "I didn't know." Too many employees feel as long as they have an excuse, it is all right to fail. Recruiters disagree. They are looking for people who have the ability to find solutions to problems and make them successes. They must see that you have the ability and desire to overcome adversity.

Look around you. Aren't there some people you know who have a tremendous ability to **make things happen**? Those individuals are goal-oriented and the kind of people we want to hire. Do what you need to do to be sure you are that kind of person. Many times, you will be faced with difficult objectives. Don't throw up your hands and quit when the going gets difficult. If you do, you won't be considered a development candidate aspiring for a top position in a major corporation. And, if your self-evaluation of your past shows that you have not "made it happen" as often as you could have, decide right now to change.

The best compliment I can hear about an applicant is, "He/she is a make-it-happen-type person." I will admit it seems some people have the ability to do it and others don't. It's one of the reasons we have to interview so many people in a year.

I remember a young man in El Paso, Texas, who had an appointment with me at 6:00 p.m. He arrived 15 minutes late. When I opened the door, he said, "I'm sorry I'm late, the traffic was bad." I didn't ask him to come in and sit down. It was obvious to me this individual thought nothing of being late because he had an excuse. I really don't know of any place, including Fredericksburg, Texas, where the traffic isn't bad at 6:00 p.m. If the person was really intent on accomplishing an objective, he would have left early to compensate for traffic. Are you a **make-it-happen** kind of person? We want to give you tough objectives and say, "Bill will get it done. Mary will get it done. Just give it to them. They will bring it back to you successfully completed."

There are a few points that I have recommended you write on your shirt cuff, the back of your hand, or certainly on a 3x5 card. One of the major points to write down is, "Have I projected to the recruiter I am a **make-it-happen**, goal-oriented, success-driven person?"

> **Ask Yourself:**
> **Am I a make-it-happen person?**
> **Do I fight through adversity**
> **to accomplish objectives?**

Enthusiasm

In addition to the basics of intellect and communication skills, recruiters look for enthusiasm. We love to see individuals who are excited to get out of bed in the morning — excited about doing whatever they have to do. It doesn't make any difference whether we're picking somebody to play bridge, throw horseshoes, play basketball, or be an employee. We like people who have sparkle in their eyes and a smile on their faces. They can laugh at themselves. They create a positive, pleasant, professional aura.

I have seen people with enthusiasm have great success and other people with even better credentials not do as well because they simply didn't have that sparkle in their eye. In interviews, I've seen enthusiasm outweigh some weaknesses. In many cases, recruiters have said, "Roger, there are some things I don't like about this applicant, but I have to tell you something. She is so enthusiastic and so upbeat that I know she is someone I would want to work with. I have absolutely no doubt we can work through a couple of the things in her background that could have been better." Therefore, when you have an interview, don't leave the enthusiasm at home, whether the interview is with Roger Cameron or a major corporate recruiter. We're all the same. We love to see enthusiastic individuals. There is no factor that assures enthusiasm in itself will get you a job, but it irons out a lot of wrinkles in an applicant's background.

And smile — a smile attracts a smile. Try it today. Try it in an interview.

Putting Success Into Words

What you've done in the past is an indication of what you'll do in the future, but I find many applicants expect us to look at their resumes and see that they've been successful in the past. If that were the case, a company would simply tell you, "Send us your resume." They would take a look at it, see your successes, and then mail you a job offer. Please understand that you must be able to communicate past successes. The key word is **communicate**.

One of the most frequent questions asked in an interview (which I answer in more detail on page 168) is: "Give me an example of a significant accomplishment. **Why** was it significant and **how** did you accomplish it?" There is probably no other question you need to spend as much time on. You must prepare one to three examples of successful achievements for both high school and college.

Remember: **Listen carefully** to the question. Was the question, "Give me **a** significant accomplishment?" or "Give me your **most** significant accomplishment," or "Give me an accomplishment in your **first job**."

Consider your **most** significant accomplishment to be a **recent** accomplishment. As you gain age and maturity, you can be expected to have more significant objectives, and, therefore, greater accomplishments. Remember, state your accomplishment in your **opening** sentence, and then support it. Be sure you illustrate your competencies as described under "Objective/Subjectice Assets" in Chapter 4. Recruiters don't want to listen to 10 minutes of verbiage before they learn what the accomplishment is.

"That's A Good Question"

You do not need to tell the recruiter that he/she has asked a good question. Unless you do it every time, the recruiter may assume that the other questions are not good questions. People say this because they are buying time while they're thinking about the answer. It is not necessary for you to say anything. Just take three to five seconds to reflect and then respond.

"How Did I Do?"

This is a very poor question. A recruiter's job is not to give you instant feedback about whether your interview was good, bad, or indifferent. We want you to know yourself. We want you to have the confidence that you have answered the questions with substance and depth, so you know yourself that the interview was a good one.

Making Eye Contact

It is critical that as you give an answer to a recruiter, you have solid eye contact with that recruiter. Have confidence in your answers. Show that confidence by looking the recruiter directly in the eye.

Often, applicants lose eye contact when it's most important — with a difficult question that may be uncomfortable to answer. That's when I see eyes go to the floor, the ceiling, or the window. You simply cannot do this.

Have you noticed that people "talk" with their eyes? Eyes can sparkle, look bland, or look suspicious. Don't you find you often make judgments based upon what you see in someone's eyes? Don't you question when someone doesn't look **you** in the eye? You may think, "Is he/she not interested, bored, uncaring, or lacking self-confidence?" Eyes should show enthusiasm, understanding, curiosity, warmth, and feeling.

Be aware of your eye contact. Where do you look when you talk to someone? Do you look at their mouth or the floor, or do you look them in the eye? If you are not accustomed to having direct eye contact, it can be awkward at first, but if you concentrate and practice, you will become comfortable with it. Eye contact should be natural, so do not "stare people down." Glance away about 10 percent of the time.

With good eye contact, **you will appear more confident and self-assured. People will listen to you and actually hear more of what you say.** Almost all of us can improve our eye contact, so make yourself conscious of yours and work to make it better.

Two Or More Recruiters

Frequently, two recruiters will interview you at the same time. Determine if both recruiters will be in the interview. If one recruiter is placed out of your normal eyesight, don't include that individual in the interview. Simply greet the recruiter at the beginning of the interview and afterwards. Be sure to remember both recruiters' names.

If you are interviewed by two recruiters, you need to maintain eye contact with both when you answer a question. However, you need to give the one who asks the question the initial and concluding eye contact. In other words, let's say Recruiter A asks you a question. Begin your answer with eye contact with Recruiter A. Continue your answer and pick up eye contact with Recruiter B. Conclude your answer with eye contact with Recruiter A. If the question is substantive and requires a lengthy answer, you may change eye contact several times, always ending by getting eye contact with the recruiter who asked the question.

Never be worried about an interview with two or more recruiters. I almost prefer it. Usually, they ask questions at the same time and that allows me the choice of which question to answer. Talk to them as you would with friends in your living room.

Always remember that companies are looking for young men and women who have poise and self-confidence. These qualities are important in group meetings as well as in one-on-one situations.

When Is An Interview Over?

The most common signal that the interview is nearing its end is when the recruiter looks at you and asks if you have any questions. Before you answer, keep two crucial considerations in mind. First, were there questions asked of you during the interview to which you responded poorly that might cause the recruiter to **rule you out**? If you've given a poor answer to a question, but the recruiter has given you very positive indications that he is going to invite you back for the follow-up interview or give you an offer, be quiet. Don't bring up a negative. I always say the quicker you get out of the room, the better off you are.

Secondly, what strong positive factors in your background were not brought out by the recruiter's questions? You might want to go back and say, "I have some questions; however, before I ask them, I feel there are some things I need to tell you about myself that weren't brought out in the interview." Do it **only** if you feel that it can have some **positive influence** on the outcome of the interview. If you already have those positive signals, don't bring up your background. Rather, get out of the interview as quickly as possible once you've asked your questions. I've seen applicants lose successful interviews because they stayed in the room and brought up irrelevant information or reminded a recruiter of a weakness that came up during the course of the interview. **Be smart.**

However, if you feel more information about you will be a positive influence, think about the answers you gave that you weren't satisfied with. If you can remember the question, restate your answer. Do it better. End on a positive note, not a negative one.

If you've missed an opportunity to give information that's important to your job pursuit, then do so at the conclusion. For example, you might say, "I've had a position similar to this one," and then give details.

Now, we come to the questions you may have. Show your intellectual curiosity by asking **high-quality** questions. You may want to re-read page 95.

These questions should reflect an accurate perception of the industry, the company, the position open, the people interviewing you, and what you want to do in your career. As I've mentioned, major corporate recruiters look for individuals who are "growable" — people who are constantly working to improve their base of knowledge in relation to their careers. These people have a high degree of curiosity, and this shows in their questions.

I recall being at a business conference with many successful people from around the country. At the start we were asked to introduce ourselves, tell where we were from, relate what our careers were, and name three people with whom we would like to have dinner. Many people said the President of the United States, a famous public figure, an actor, a politician, etc. But, as I listened to everyone, I thought, "Is that what would really be important to me?"

I was the last to get up. I told the group that the three people with whom I'd most like to have dinner would be people who were **full of curiosity.** I didn't care if they were plumbers or carpenters or housekeepers. It made no difference. I knew I'd enjoy an extremely interesting dinner if I were simply with people who exhibited a high degree of curiosity.

Corporations want to hire people who are curious, who ask questions, and who are interested in what's happening. Don't hesitate to ask questions when they are requested because they are central to proving you are a curious person.

Closing The Interview

Close the interview by being **upbeat**. If you have a high degree of interest in the company and in the position, let the recruiter know that. However, do not tell the recruiter you have a strong interest if you don't. There are going to be times when you interview with a high quality company which, for one reason or another, just does not fit with your career goals at the time. You should not mislead the recruiter by overstating your interest.

Let me say again that if you have an interest in the company, you cannot afford to walk out of the interview without showing a high degree of interest. You must make your close **personal** and **specific**. Make a statement that could **only** be relevant to this company. For instance, "I have a strong interest in Quaker Oats. I was impressed by many things, but most of all by the statements your president and CEO, Mr. William D. Smithburg, made in your 1991 annual report beginning on page 2. I'm impressed with your sole concentration on grocery products and your concept of 'controllable earnings.' I look forward to having another interview with your company or to receiving an offer from your company (depending on where you are in the interviewing procedure)." This response needs to be **sincere** and **upbeat**. Notice this statement could not be made about another company. Someone else wouldn't even know what you were talking about. This is the true test of a good close. You may not have a lot of time for a close, yet you **must** deliver it. Have your points well-ingrained in your mind for fluid and believable delivery.

Sometimes, an applicant just doesn't know **when** to get out of an interview. If you have a positive response to your statement of interest in the company and the interviewer says, "I'm very excited about what I see. We'd like to invite you for a follow-up interview," then, it's time to get up and leave.

Sending Thank-You Notes
Following your initial interview, be sure to write thank-you notes to those companies that have expressed an interest in pursuing you further. The purpose of sending such a note is to restate your strong

interest in the company and your desire for a follow-up interview. To help you with this task, here are some guidelines.

1) Using quality plain paper, you can either write or type your notes. If your handwriting or printing is not neat, you should type your letters on a computer with a quality printer or a good typewriter. Pay close attention to your spelling, sentence structure, grammar, and punctuation. Mistakes in these areas will ruin the message you are trying to convey. In fact, it could reverse a positive interview. Be very careful about managing the details of writing and sending your thank-you letters. Proof every line of type, and be sure you send the correct letters to the right people. I recall a young man who sent Company A's thank-you letter to Company B and vice versa. Both companies declined him.

2) **Never** ask a question in your letter that forces a recruiter to respond to your letter. You want to motivate him to take action and make arrangements for the next step, not increase his paperwork.

3) Write your letters immediately and send them no later than the weekend after the interview is over. Other applicants will be sending their thank-you notes promptly, and if yours is delayed, the company could assume a lack of interest on your part.

4) **Do** tell a company when you have chosen them as one of your top companies. Remember how good you feel when you know someone thinks highly of you.

5) Do not start your letter thanking a company for taking the time to interview you. Instead, focus on how much you enjoyed the time spent with the recruiter learning more about the company and the positions discussed.

6) Tailor each letter to each individual company. A form letter will do you more harm than good. A personalized letter expresses the **sincere** interest you have in a particular company. Take a few moments to reflect on the interview and determine why you are excited about that company. Then, create a letter that will communicate your desire for follow-up interviews and inspire the recruiter to pursue you further.

7) If, because of your availability or other reasons, a company has not started pursuit within 30 days of the initial interview, you should send another note. Again, you should reiterate your interest and confirm your date of availability.

8) I want to caution you. Please realize the massive amount of mail that any corporate recruiter or department manager gets in a day. Why not try to be unique in sending a piece of mail? What's wrong with sending an envelope that is a different color? I just wonder — if I received 20 pieces of mail in the morning and 19 of them were white and one of them was red — wouldn't the red one catch my eye? Have you ever received a telegram and not opened it immediately? Did you ever receive an overnight letter and not immediately want to know what it was and open it? I remember one time that I opened the mail and out rolled what looked like a stick of dynamite. It actually was a red paper tube with a fuse sticking out the top. Ingenious. Unique. And you can bet it was absolutely the first piece of mail I picked up and opened. As a matter of fact, several years have passed and I still have the container. Please don't be afraid to be professionally unique. Create your own marketing methods. Recruiters like innovative and creative approaches rather than funny or silly ones. We're not talking about that kind of approach.

Follow-Up Interviews

I have observed applicants work very hard and become very competitive in their initial interviews. They are invited for follow-up interviews and think they're over the hump and on the downhill side. You are **never** on the downhill side until you have an offer. I've seen too many times when a sports team was out in front. It appeared obvious to them they would win, and then they let up. The next thing you know, they were defeated. You may have had this happen to you sometime in your own life. You knew you were in a winning situation. Suddenly, you found yourself defeated. **When you prepare for a follow-up interview, prepare even harder than you did for your initial interviews.**

I have been excited about applicants I've accepted and looked forward to introducing them to some of my client companies. Three months later, I would go to their particular location to better prepare them for interviewing, but this time they just wouldn't impress me. Why? They knew they had been accepted. They assumed once they were accepted, they could never be declined, which is certainly not true. You can never let up. You can never feel you are home safe until the offer to go to work for a company is in your pocket.

Normally, if you have impressed a recruiter sufficiently in a preliminary interview, you'll go through a series of follow-up interviews. You could receive as little as 24 hours notice of an interview trip, and you need to be ready. Get your suits and your "professional casual" travel clothes cleaned and pressed, shine your shoes, and ensure your travel essentials are easily accessible. Also, organize your corporate information, and keep it handy.

Here are some broad guidelines to follow when a company calls you:

- **Take notes.** Write down **everything**. Take the name, number, and title/job of the person calling if you don't know him/her. Write down any specific information that is given. Ideally, take notes on or in your calendar or datebook.

- **Don't assume.** Applicants have been brought in for jobs or locations that were different from those discussed. Company representatives (particularly if they are human resources/recruiting assistants) may not have complete information about you, and they may assume, for example, that you know they are in a certain location when you really do not know their location.

- **Ask questions.** Verify what you "think." The person with whom you are speaking may "only want answers to two quick questions," yet may have all kinds of information that would be helpful to you.

- **Close the call.** At the end of the call, confirm you have correctly recorded all the details and verify what (if anything) you will have to do next: make reservations, call the company back after checking on something, etc. Also, find out what **the company** will be doing to set up your logistics.

- **Be your smart self.** The person calling could be your future boss! Show energy, enthusiasm, and appreciation for his/her continued interest. Don't burn your bridges.

Between your notification of an interview and your briefing, you must increase your level of knowledge of the industry, company, and position for which you are interviewing. Quality companies have come to consider a lack of such effort to be indicative of either a lack of interest or a lack of follow-through, both of which are **dangerous**. You should read any books you have not yet finished and also find the best library to do general industry reading and company research.

If you know the location for which you are being considered, call the local Chamber of Commerce and have them send you information. Look up specifics in the library, too. Below are some industries that lend themselves easily to research you can do right away:

- **Medical instrument companies** — Go to hospitals and speak with doctors, surgeons, and purchasing agents. (Wear your suit for these meetings.) Tell them that you are interviewing for a position with Company XYZ. Ask what they like and don't like about the company product. Is the price competitive? Is the quality consistent? Are they pleased with the sales representative? What is the competition doing better or worse?

- **Pharmaceutical companies** — Visit pharmacies and doctors. If you are interviewing for a sales position, go to non-chain drugstores where the pharmacists will have purchasing decisions. As with the medical companies, ask questions to understand the company's reputation and the quality of their product.

- **Consumer products** — Visit grocery stores and try to speak with the managers about the company's product and the competition. Where is the product located on the shelves? How is it priced? What colors and print do they use in the packaging? Ask customers you see at the stores why they chose or did not choose the product. Check out the Sunday paper for coupons. What do you notice about the color, expiration date, and discount amount? Watch for all advertisements in the media. See if you can speak with the local sales representative.

- **Retail stores or distribution centers** — Visit local stores, if possible. Try to speak with the managers. How are the stores laid out? Do you feel welcome? How are the items merchandised? Are the stores light and bright? How are the prices? Ask questions about the transportation departments. How often is merchandise delivered? What are the top selling items?

- **Quick service restaurants** — Do some market research. Visit the local restaurants and their competition. Analyze the prices, the menu selection, and the variety. How happy are the employees? How clean are the restaurants? How long are you kept waiting? How are the restaurants being advertised? What are the coupons, commercials, and signs on the windows like? Where are the locations? Are they a drive-in, eat-in, or take-out restaurants only? What works? What would you want to change?

Once you have been invited on a follow-up interview, the first thing you need to do is to ensure that you have all your travel logistics completely arranged and that you understand how you will be getting from place to place. If you will be traveling by air, the company may send your tickets in the mail or, depending on any timing constraints, perhaps by an overnight mail service. If you are flying with an airline and are a member of that airline's frequent flyer program, be sure to get proper credit for your flight. If you don't belong, be sure to sign up before the flight! If the tickets will be pre-paid at the airport, you **must** be at the airport at least one hour prior to departure with two types of picture identification. Some companies will ask you to purchase your own tickets and will reimburse you. In this case, you will usually complete an expense report and will be reimbursed before you receive the bill from your credit card company. Remember that airline tickets are the same as money. You should never discard unused portions of your ticket, and you should keep the copies for receipts. If a company asks you to make your own airline reservations, do not book reservations with penalties which restrict changes. On occasion, it will be necessary or preferred to arrange the follow-up interviews of two separate companies on back-to-back days, possibly combining the travel plans. It is very important that you take extreme care to divide costs fairly between the companies involved. You should **never** see one company on another company's money.

If you will be traveling by car, make sure you have precise directions to prevent you from getting lost and being late. **Always** try to arrive at your destination no later than 6:00 p.m. to ensure you will get in early enough to relax and get a full night's sleep.

Now that you have all of your travel arrangements confirmed, you need to verify that every step in the process is covered. "Every step" means your transportation from

1) **Your home to airport.** You may be driving yourself to the airport in your own car, or perhaps your spouse or a friend will drop you off. Whatever your means of transportation, plan ahead so that you make it to the airport **at least** one hour prior to your flight departure time. Don't let yourself get into a "traffic jam." If you do you will be rushing to make your flight, and you will be nervous before you even start your journey. I have seen applicants miss their flights due to poor planning, which showed nothing to the company but that they lacked good judgment. Plan ahead for traffic congestion, gas purchases, a full parking lot, or any other "problem" that might come up that would delay or prevent you from arriving at your flight on time to board the plane.

2) **Airport to airport.** If you are going to have a layover, determine how much time you have between flights. If your first flight had any delays, will that cause you to miss your next flight, and if so, what will your strategy be then? For example, let's say you know you have a 45-minute layover in the Atlanta airport. When you arrive at your boarding gate at the point of origin, ask the attendant for the number of the gate at which you will be arriving in Atlanta, and the number of the gate from which you will be departing. By doing this, you will know if a short walk or a fast run is required to reach your next plane. If there will be a distance between gates, ask someone if a shuttle bus is available and if it can speed up your time. Always carry all necessary phone numbers with you in case a situation develops that may cause a delay while you are in transit.

Also, before you leave on your trip, get the phone number of the hotel at which you are staying. You never know what might occur while you are traveling. If your connecting flight is cancelled or if you have any other difficulties during travel, you should leave a message at the hotel's front desk explaining your situation for the person meeting you. As a basic rule, hotel rooms are held until 6:00 p.m. for the arriving guest. To guarantee your room for a late arrival, you will need to give a credit card number to the reservation desk. Therefore, when you get details for your hotel, be sure to get the confirmation number and verify that the room will be held for late arrival. If you will be unable to arrive as planned due to a cancelled flight, you must call the hotel prior to 6:00 p.m. and get a cancellation number. Otherwise, the company on your credit card will be charged!

3) **Airport to hotel.** When you confirm your travel arrangements, be sure to find out who will be picking you up at the airport. Will it be a taxi? A limo service? Will there be a company representative there for you? If so, what should you wear? And where will you be met? At the gate? Baggage claim? The curb outside Terminal 1? Will you know what this person meeting you looks like and what he or she will be wearing? Or will he or she be holding a sign that has your name on it?

You may be picking up a rental car at the aiport. If so, you must have a valid credit card issued with your name on it and available credit. You must also have a current driver's license. And be aware that car rental companies have rules that restrict them from renting to individuals unless they meet certain age qualifications. Check with some of the major rental companies to determine current regulations. If you do have to rent a car, determine how you will get to the hotel from the airport. You must have detailed instructions in hand prior to getting in that car so that you know where you are going. Always carry the phone number of the hotel at which you will be staying. Your hotel reservations will usually be made by the company, but, occasionally, alternative directions will be given to you. Your hotel costs may be billed directly to the company, or the company may ask you to pay and will reimburse you. Again, you will usually complete an expense report.

4) **Hotel to company.** Determine if a company representative will pick you up, and if so, what time. If you must drive to the company, do you have accurate directions? How long will it take to get there? Should you do a test run to make sure there are no detours or other obstacles? Where will you meet the company representative? In the lobby of the hotel? Outside? Who will it be? Have you met him or her before? Even if this individual may not participate in your actual "interview," he or she will still be evaluating you and forming an opinion of you.

Do not leave out one step. Make sure you can address each step so you don't get to the airport in the middle of the night and realize nobody told you how you were supposed to get to the hotel. If you are given an itinerary over the phone, go over it mentally **before** you hang up. Also, take $100 cash with you, and keep all your receipts so you can get fully reimbursed. **Carry on your luggage.** You **don't** want to arrive without your interview suit and toiletries. It has happened before. **Don't let it happen to you!**

Items to bring to your follow-up interview.
1) Your resume
2) Company literature
3) *Your Career Fast Track*
4) Three personal and three professional references, including names, addresses, and phone numbers

Start preparing for your follow-up interview no later than one night before the interview is to take place. Then, on your flight you can review all of the material one more time so that you will thoroughly understand the information. Review all of the information listed above to maximize your chances for success.

You may think you are an interviewing expert now. You are not because you have only become good at initial interviews, not follow-ups. While you should be quite confident, there are some areas you have not been exposed to that might occur.

When hiring a development candidate, most companies today will want a unanimous decision — having all managers say "thumbs up" on an applicant. It is not good to have even one manager say "no" to you when, in fact, you might one day work for that individual. It doesn't create the best working environment. Every person with whom you interview is an important person in getting an offer from that company. Make each person feel he/she is important to the decision. You must go to each interview armed with questions for that interviewer. The follow-up interview is one of the most important moves you're going to make in your career.

Wrap up every interview in a positive manner. During the follow-up interview, **tell the recruiter you want an offer.** I don't care what the words are. I don't care how you do it. Too many times, you will find the **time** and the **desire** to close those "friendly" interviews, but the tough interviews will remain unclosed for some inexcusable reason. **Stop** right now and tell yourself you're going to close **every** interview equally.

I've had applicants return from an interview and say, "Roger, I couldn't close because we ran out of time," or some other such excuse. When I find they didn't close the interview, I tell the applicants, "Look, there's no reason for me to explain how to do something if you're not going to listen." The applicants say to me, "Roger, you know the interview went up to the last second, and I didn't have time to close the interview in an upbeat manner." I always reply, "I don't want to hear about it. I don't care if you have to throw your body at the foot of the door before you leave somebody's office. **You must close that interview.**"

You must have the ability to tell a recruiter, "Look, I've got to tell you something. I'm very excited about your company. I gained my excitement by having my first interview, reading the literature, and talking to other people who are working for your company." (Remember, make a statement that is **only** relevant to that company.) "I'm looking forward to receiving an offer from your company." Or, you can say, "This is my choice — the company I want to work for. I want you to know I'm looking forward to receiving an offer from your company and accepting it." I don't care how you do it. **You've got to do it before you leave the interview.** That recruiter may be interviewing three or four different applicants. If three of them have stated an interest and one doesn't, you can bet the one who doesn't is **not** going to pull the offer. Exceptions are rare. You wouldn't want to roll the dice for the exception.

Once again, I want to remind you of professionalism. If you cannot see yourself working in this company, or if the position is not right for you, don't mislead the company or the recruiters. Thank them for the follow-up interview. Tell them you appreciate their giving you a better look at what the position and the company is all about, but it is not right for you. Don't have them make the offer to you and turn down other applicants who have a very strong interest in the position. If you're not sure this is the company you want to work for, be careful what you tell them. You must later be able to live with the comments you make. Be professional. Corporate America is a small world. You want to be proud of your ethics and professionalism should you ever run into employees of the company or the recruiter later. **Never burn a bridge when it is not necessary.**

A follow-up interview may include a tour of the manufacturing plant. You must get involved by exhibiting a high degree of interest and curiosity. Don't be afraid to ask permission to cross safety lines to take a closer look at a piece of equipment. Ask numerous questions about what you see. One of the most fascinating experiences in the world is to go through a major manufacturing facility. I'm not an engineer, but I'm always overwhelmed by what great engineers have done in different manufacturing processes. Manufacturing plants are fascinating. You must show excitement about being there and learning about the processes. Manufacturing people are proud of their efforts, and you must show enthusiasm for the plant environment as well.

I have seen an applicant go through a plant and have the person who was taking him on the tour introduce him to a laborer on the floor. The tour guide then said, "Oh, by the way, excuse me a minute; I see someone over here I need to speak with. I'll be right back." The company was one that emphasized participative management, and they watched the applicant to see if he developed a conversation with that worker. If you find yourself in a similar situation, not only develop a conversation, but also remember the individual's name.

Imagine a situation in which you have been taken to a recruiter's office in a manufacturing facility. The recruiter has taken her name plaque off her desk. She introduces herself to you when you come in. When your interview is over, she shakes hands with you, looks you in the eye, and says, "What's my name?" If you've written her name in your spiral notebook as I suggested, you're more likely to remember it. Another helpful technique is to be sure to use her name two or three times during the interview. This kind of situation does happen. If you are aware that it might, you can be prepared.

If you are interviewing for a sales position, as a part of the follow-up process, you will probably be invited to spend a day in the field with a local sales representative. Remember, this person is doing you a favor by taking extra time from his/her schedule to show you the job. Be extremely polite and considerate. Arrive at the agreed-upon destination 15 minutes early. Come dressed in your best interviewing suit, unless other attire is specifically requested. (Special Note: If you are going into a hospital where you may tour surgery areas, ask if you will need tennis shoes.) If you meet for a meal, there is no need to offer to pay, as the sales representative will put it on an expense report. However, it is important to thank your host. **You must get involved. This is not a time for you to simply follow along behind and not interact. Remember, you are being evaluated.** Do whatever you can to help out and make the sales representative's day easier. Offer to carry a briefcase, park the car, or anything else you think would be helpful. Make **elaborate** notes of each account on which you call. Who was called on? For what purpose? Write down questions you have of the sales technique used or questions asked and responses. Do not do anything to interfere negatively with the sales calls. Your social skills will be observed and noted. Be polite and friendly but not obtrusive. When you are back in the car driving to the next sales call, then is the time to demonstrate your curiosity and insight by asking good questions. At the end of the day, remember to ask for the sales representative's card. Then, call and/or write to thank him/her again for the valuable time that was spent with you. It is up to you to make that individual comfortable about referring you on to the next step.

I have watched applicants spend a day in the field with a sales representative. Never once did they offer to help carry the sales person's briefcase. They never asked questions and did not even take notes. They forgot the clients they met. Don't be guilty of this kind of behavior. You must show involvement. You're not out there simply for the sake of observation. You're out there for the company to see what your interest is in the position. Be able to show your intelligence and how you perceive the position, the industry, and the company through the questions you ask.

Frequently, I have observed applicants pass up the opportunity to show interest in a company product. Many recruiters bring their products to an interview or display them in their offices. For you not to mention the products or ask questions about them is an interviewing error from which you may not recover. I remember an applicant who interviewed with PepsiCo and turned down a Pepsi offered by the recruiter. Another applicant failed to show any interest in a fascinating display of surgical instruments lying on a recruiter's desk. There is no way to justify these foolish actions. It's a shame to ruin your chances for an offer in the final interview by not staying constantly alert and thoroughly involved. The minute you're on company money, you'd better be focused totally on that company. The minute you walk out the door at home, the company is paying every penny of your expenses, so it is only appropriate for you to give them every ounce of your concentration.

See Appendix D for a self-evaluation to use after each interview.

CHAPTER 7

"Roger Cameron is right on target when it comes to knowing what's required to get ahead in today's competitive environment. The choices you make now while in college or preparing for college will have a significant impact on your career. Remember, one thing no one can take from you is your education — so choose it wisely."

—Troy McMahon
Engineering
General Mills, Inc.

CHAPTER 7

Face The Big Questions —
Develop The Best Answers

Probably the best learning experience an applicant could have would be to sit in the corner of my hotel room and listen to other applicants interviewing. Members of my staff have watched and listened to me conduct interviews. They will each tell you they were amazed at what they saw applicants do and not do and their demeanor throughout the course of an interview, not to mention some of their answers.

Many applicants approach recruiters as if they're carrying the weight of the world on their shoulders. We want someone to walk in relaxed and not afraid to smile. One of the best techniques to help you relax and be confident is visualization. Top athletes find it to be an extremely effective tool. You can, too. Prior to an interview, stretch out in a chair or on the bed and visualize the **perfect** interview. See yourself walking through the door with poise and confidence, giving a solid handshake, making good eye contact, giving a warm smile, and saying the recruiter's name in an enthusiastic way and with a well-modulated voice. Visualize yourself with good posture as you sit down and listen actively to the recruiter. Most importantly, see yourself articulating answers with substance, conciseness, and enthusiasm.

I encourage you to make visualization a habit. It is a very effective technique. After all, if the experts do it, why shouldn't you? When you interview, put a smile on the face of a recruiter. Be eager to be there. Make the conversation flow. While we certainly understand you undoubtedly have some butterflies in your stomach, attempt to show a light, relaxed, professional style.

It's crucial to understand the two basic philosophies which are the foundation blocks for probably 90 percent of the questions you will be asked.

- **Philosophy #1** — Companies judge success by the accomplishment of objective. Whether we are a derelict in the park or president of the U.S., we each have objectives. Because we are unique individuals, our objectives are different. Some objectives are more difficult to achieve than others and, therefore, are more significant successes when accomplished.

When you are interviewing, keep in mind this concept about accomplishing objectives successfully. Remember that you can have a slight failure or a catastrophic failure, a small success or a phenomenal success. In giving answers to interview questions, do not state the **degree** of success. Verbalize the success in such a way that the **recruiter** can determine the degree of success or failure.

- **Philosophy #2** — Everybody can improve. You should always project a high capacity for and interest in professional growth. Many interview questions will address your attitude about constructive comments from management. Some people are difficult to manage. Fortune 500 companies do not need to hire management problems. They want people who are team players and who respond well to management.

Recruiters will ask this question frequently, "If you take all the assets you have and use on a daily basis, which ones do you feel you **can** improve?" The key word is **can**. The attitude that we're looking for in applicants is that they can improve everything they're doing and would hope to be able to do so even at age 98. You can give an excellent speech, but you can give an even better speech. You can be a good sorority president, but you can become even better. You can run a four-minute mile, but you can run an even faster mile. We look for people with great attitudes about expanding themselves.

When you are asked a question, you need to listen carefully to each word in the question. Understand the difference between the words **can** and **need**. **Can** is used to refer to your attitude to grow. **Need** is used to refer to a weakness or a less than strength as defined under weaknesses on page 87. The question, "Which one of your assets do you feel you **need** to improve?" can give you some difficulty. **Need**, by definition, means that you have a significant weakness in that area. I can't imagine Procter & Gamble, Mobil Oil, or any other great company coming to me and saying, "Roger, travel around the world and let us pay you $8,000 to $10,000 to hire an individual who has weaknesses." You must always be honest. If you have deficiencies, you need to be willing and able to talk about those deficiencies. Hopefully, you're doing something about them. You can point out a program you are in at that very moment which is helping you bring the deficiency up to a strength.

Know yourself. Know your strengths and your weaknesses. Feel comfortable in being able to talk about them knowing when you put the strengths on the scale, they will far outweigh any weaknesses you might have.

Interviewing In The First Person

Be sure to reply to the interviewer in the first person. You show lack of decisiveness and confidence to reply in the second person as if you were speaking of a third party instead of yourself.

Sometimes, an applicant says, "I feel that's what **a person** should do." We're not hiring a third party, we're hiring **you**. You must talk in the **first** person.

You're going into an interview to be evaluated for **your** abilities to accomplish difficult objectives and motivate people. **You** must tell us that in the first person, and there can be no exception.

Remember, we're not having a philosophical conversation. In that case, we could use the second person, but in an interview the entire objective is to determine whether or not to offer **you** a job. The first person usage is critical to **your** success.

Listen to others around you talk. Notice how often they slide into the second person. As you're interviewing with Corporate America, you must know how we talk. Listen carefully to the examples you put on your tape recorder. If you use the second person excessively, it will be a factor to rule you out.

In interviews you must individualize your accomplishments. Recruiters expect to hear you say "I." Otherwise, they have no ability to know what you accomplish versus what someone else accomplishes. **Be careful in wording your accomplishments. You must demonstrate the ability to be an individual and yet be a team player.** I know of no company in America that will hire an individual who is not a team player. Corporations want people who can interact with others, whether they are subordinates, peers, or superiors. In today's participative world, you must come across strongly as a team player.

"Tell Me About Yourself"

The recruiter says to you, **"Tell me about yourself."** There will rarely be an interview when that question is not asked. Too many applicants feel this is a license to bore the recruiter. I have had applicants use the entire 30-minute interview telling me about themselves but not covering the issues in which I had any interest. Some interviewing books encourage you to take 20 to 40 minutes for your answer. I disagree. I feel you should talk no more than two to three minutes about high school achievements and the same about college achievements. In your answer, there are only two factors you should cover — your goals and your accomplishments.

When interviewers ask this question, they are attempting to determine if you are at the "helm" of your vehicle (your personal life). They want to be assured you're solidly in the front seat, behind the steering wheel making sure you're "driving" your life in the direction you want it to go. Too many people appear to ride on the passenger side and, sadly, some seem to be riding in the trunk. There are only **three** words that can give the proper perspective to a recruiter — **want, goal,** or **objective.** These three words closely state you are in control of your life and are working to make your life successful. We recognize that you'll expect to be put in charge of a unit, department, or division of the company you join, and we want to feel confident you'll, by nature, step to the "helm" of that unit.

I'll give you an example of an individual who had no understanding of the need to direct his life by first discovering his own wants and goals and then acting upon them decisively. A short time ago, I interviewed a young development candidate. His spouse was also present during the interview. About 20 minutes into the interview, I sensed his spouse becoming "uptight." She crossed her arms, leaned back in the chair, and arched her back — all signs of tensing up. I wasn't quite sure what was causing it, even though I hoped I wasn't giving her any cause to be upset. Suddenly, she interrupted the interview in an explosive manner, looked at her husband, and in a fierce voice, asked him if he had ever made a decision on his own! Then she said, "I can tell you, I wouldn't hire you!"

I admit I was uncomfortable observing this scenario but not as uncomfortable as I would have been if I had been riding down in the elevator with them after I proceeded to rule her husband out.

Let's take a look at the interview. I was using the "Why?" interview as described in the next topic. I asked the applicant why he chose his college. He told me that he had never planned to go to college, but two of his best friends talked him into going and so he went where they went. I asked why he selected biology as his major. He really didn't know what he wanted to do, but because he had a good friend whom he respected who chose biology, he though it would be good for him also. I then asked why he joined a fraternity and, again, it was because of a friend. This applicant's direction in school and in life reflected no want, goal, or objective.

Here is an example of an appropriate reply given by an individual who was asked to tell about himself: "I'm an only child of a Texas ranch family. When I went to high school, there were several things I **wanted to** accomplish. First of all, I wanted a grade point average (goal) that would allow me to get into the college of my choice (accomplishment). I also knew that I wanted to play sports (goal). I was a wrestler and a football player (accomplishment)." Remember, we're taking a hard look to see if you are goal-oriented and have the ability to **make it happen**! Notice I didn't say goal, accomplishment, **detail**. At this point, you will not be going into detail as to why you set the goal or how you accomplished it.

As you discuss a point of interest, recruiters may interrupt to ask questions. They will want to know why that goal was important to you and how you accomplished it. Be sensitive to recruiters and allow them to enter in. This approach allows them to ask you to elaborate on a point of interest that is important to them.

When you are interrupted, it's critical that you remember exactly where you were when interrupted, so when you finish answering a recruiter's question, you can come back smoothly, picking up where you left off. You **should never** look at the recruiter after elaborating on a point and say, "Now, where was I?" After all, it is your story.

Answering The "Why?" Questions

"Why?" is the **most frequently** asked question facing any applicant. I want to remind you that we're looking for development candidates. Development candidates are ultimately going to spend the bulk of their days making decisions. We ask, **"Why?" to determine how you think and reason and to determine your ability to achieve a quality conclusion.** Everyone reaches conclusions, but few people consistently reach **quality** conclusions. The recruiter will look for the steps you take to reach a conclusion.

Remember that both you and the company want you to achieve as much as you can in management. In order to do this, you will have to demonstrate logical thinking skills and good judgment in reaching conclusions. When you answer "Why?" questions, strive to show the recruiter the logical steps that are leading you to your conclusions. Recruiters want managers who are independent thinkers.

The recruiter may ask you why you took actions or made certain choices in a number of key areas. Why did you choose that college? Why that curriculum? Why that GPA? Why sports? Why sorority? Why do you want this position?

The best approach to any **"Why?"** question is to think in terms of a **comparison.** Compare the positives and negatives of the choice you made with the positives and negatives of your other options. Do this concisely and **without** rambling.

Tell us, for example, the options you had in financing college — borrowing money from family members or a bank, getting work, or winning a scholarship. Perhaps you planned on ROTC being a big part of your college career. Let us know you analyzed all those factors before you came to a decision. I often ask military officers why they enrolled in the ROTC program. The most frequent response I get is because their parents couldn't afford to send them through college. That suggests to the recruiter that if you can't get into ROTC, you can't graduate from college. Well, I just don't agree with that. There are other ways to finance your education.

I sometimes ask applicants why they selected their majors. One applicant was a history major and to my question, "Why did you major in history?" replied, "Well, I wanted to go to law school." I said, "Well, what happened to the objective of being a lawyer?" He replied, "Oh, I changed my mind." The applicant was being evasive or didn't know how to show me the way he thinks and how he came to this conclusion. He missed a great opportunity to demonstrate logical thinking skills—a key qualification for managers. Therefore, understand the critical nature of your ability to handle a **"Why?"** question. Many recruiters will give you nothing but a **"Why?"** interview. The key here is to let us know each step in your thinking process in a very succinct manner.

An excellent exercise is to take all the major events in your life and write them down. Then, ask a **"Why?"** question about each event. Use a tape recorder to answer. Then, listen to yourself. Does what you say show strong reasoning? If it does, you're in good shape for interviewing. **Stop** — practice this exercise now.

Answering Education Questions

If you have a degree that is generally considered irrelevant to business, such as liberal arts, the question is not whether you should or should not have chosen it. The question is, "How do you sell it to Corporate America?" You and I both know that some of the top people in Corporate America have liberal arts degrees, but I've never had a company ask me to find them a candidate with a degree in liberal arts. It's perfectly all right that you have one. No one would suggest that you couldn't get value out of it. Yet, it is not directly relevant to the functions in Corporate America. You'll have to handle objections to an irrelevant degree in an interview.

Don't get defensive about your liberal arts degree. We're not suggesting you wasted your time in college or that you will get no value from it. However, it seems I spend half my time consoling people who have this degree. I want to help you get over the fact that it is an irrelevant degree. It was not designed for Corporate America, for the world of profit. It isn't related to finance, data processing, engineering, business, accounting, etc. — those areas directly linked to Corporate America.

Here's how you might explain it: "Relative to my decision today to obtain a position in Corporate America, my liberal arts degree was a mistake. I don't want to suggest that I didn't get things out of political science that will be of value to me, because I thoroughly enjoyed it and feel I developed skills important in the business world, such as problem-solving and communication skills. However, had I known then that I wanted a career in the profit-oriented world, I would have earned a more relevant degree."

Stress your determination to enter the business world. Frequently, in asking candidates why they want to go into business when they have a liberal arts degree, I have to say, "You've never shown any indication of interest in business in the 21+ years of your life," and I draw an analogy. I ask the applicant to assume he has a neighbor who has lived next door for 20 years. He has left the house every morning and returned every night, but he has never looked across the fence and said hello. Then, suddenly, one day, he leans across the fence and asks the neighbor to marry him. The neighbor answers, "For 20 years you've ignored me. Now you want to marry me. Why?" The neighbor has every reason to ask, and she needs an explanation. The applicant has to have a rationale. He can't just say, "Sally no longer interests me; therefore, I'm coming to you."

You're going to have to tell Corporate America how you decided you wanted a career in industry. Give evidence of research you did, books you read, people with whom you spoke, and choices you considered.

I remember interviewing an individual with a government degree. I said, "Government degree. I just don't know what I can do." But, he wasn't about to accept no for an answer. He went on to give me very solid **proof** of his interest. "The reason I'm interested in Corporate America is that I have read several books (he stated title and author) about business which have encouraged me to make this choice for my career. I have talked with a friend in a major corporation who is responsible for (name of function). For the following reasons (he put his fingers up in the air and ticked them off), I have decided to go into Corporate America." I listened to him. There was absolutely no question in my mind this young man had done his homework. He was committed and convincing. I brought him to recruiters, and every company fought over him. He now has an outstanding job in industry, is performing at an outstanding level, and has remained a close friend.

Recruiters don't care whether you have an irrelevant degree. They **do** care whether you are coming to us for the right reasons. You're bringing **proof and evidence** of those reasons, not simply rhetoric.

Accomplishments Deserve Full Answers

As I have previously stated on developing your resume in Chapter 3, **no question will be more important than, "Tell me about a significant accomplishment."** After all, if you can't talk about past accomplishments, there is no reason to believe you can talk about future accomplishments. Normally, the way the question will be asked is, "Tell me about a significant accomplishment and how you accomplished it." Be very careful to answer all three parts of this key question about an accomplishment. Do you see the third part? Two are choices: tell about the accomplishment, and tell how you accomplished it. The third part is to tell how it was significant.

Often, when I ask an applicant this question, I'll wait two or three minutes to find out what the accomplishment actually is! **You should identify the accomplishment in your opening statement**. The example you give should be an accomplishment with an **impact** on your mission. Take the time to **develop the significance**. Tell how your accomplishment had a major effect on the overall status of the mission.

Don't tell the recruiter that the accomplishment was important or significant. **Describe why** it was important and significant. Your answer should **demonstrate** the significance.

I remember a trip I made to do some final interviewing. I had sent a letter to approximately 30 applicants asking them to be prepared to tell me about a significant accomplishment, why it was significant, and how they accomplished it. Each one of them knew this question was very important for a successful interview. It was obvious that each had worked very hard to be prepared. But this was interesting: As hard as they worked, I did not have one applicant get this question right. Not one. Everyone wanted to tell me what the accomplishment was and then tell me how they accomplished it. No one took the time to elaborate on the **significance** of the accomplishment itself.

One young man in field artillery said to me, "Roger, I was given the task of designing a new firing system for our field artillery unit." I said, "Insignificant issue." He said, "Roger, I've got to tell you something. If that's insignificant, I have never done anything significant." I said, "Let me show you how I would handle it." I continued, "This event occurred while I was stationed in Germany (we consider that to be the most eastern defensive line of the United States). If we were going to run into a conflict at that time, it was probably going to come from across the Russian border. My job was to design a new firing system. In the event of a conflict, it is the field artillery's job to put steel on the target accurately before we are run over. If we don't put steel accurately on the target, that is exactly what will happen." You see, if he had established this from the beginning, I could have seen the importance of what he was doing. You must understand the importance of establishing the significance of your accomplishments.

We in Corporate America are not going to buy rhetoric. We want to see the explanation of the accomplishment's importance, difficulty, or significance. We must see evidence.

Your answer must include behavioral traits, characteristics, and competencies that enabled you to achieve your objective. This issue is duscussed in depth on page 180. They should show that you:
- Were organized.
- Knew priorities.
- Found solutions to unexpected problems.
- Were creative, innovative, resourceful.
- Interacted well with peers, superiors, and subordinates.
- Managed time effectively.
- Were goal-oriented.
- Were able to break a goal down into parts, assigning those parts to others responsible for this objective's success.
- Brought the work to a conclusion. Be sure to mention if you brought the project in on budget and/or on time and how that had an **impact on the project.**

Don't be in a rush to answer this crucial question. It's one of the most important questions you'll be asked in an interview. And you **will** be asked. You can be certain that you'll be asked for **numerous** examples.

Problem Solving
A similar question is, "Tell me about a significant **problem** you solved, why it was significant, and **how** you solved it." Usually, this

doesn't mean a people problem. It's a problem that had impact on the objective. Again, without fail, you must bring out your consistent behavioral traits.

Search your past to identify the most relevant problems and accomplishments related to objectives you tried to accomplish for part-time work, social clubs, or other groups.

"What Is Your Leadership Style?"

This question may be phrased in other ways, such as, "How do you get people to work for you?" or "How do you motivate others?" or "Why do people want to work for you?" As a student you may have never supervised others. If recruiters ask you to tell them about your leadership style, you will have to tell them you haven't had a supervisory position. However, you will need to think seriously about what your leadership style should be so that you will be prepared in the interview to tell recruiters how you **would** supervise others.

You have probably discovered that participative management is strongly encouraged in many corporations in the U.S. today. This management style requires that everyone from the bottom to the top of an organization has input into processes and procedures. Therefore, you need to study the participative management concept thoroughly and be able to discuss it with recruiters. There are many books and periodicals that can give you information. You will find the following steps are important in this management style. Include them when you discuss what you would do as a supervisor.

1) Analyze clearly the objective given you.
2) **Explain** (not tell) it to your subordinates.
3) Ask for their input.
4) **Listen** to their ideas and suggestions.
5) Incorporate these ideas with yours.
6) Delegate responsibility.

7) Allow your people to perform (realizing there are many right ways to accomplish an objective).

A supervisor's ability to **motivate** people is most important to corporations. Observe managers you know who motivate others well. Read books, go to seminars, and listen to tapes on the subject so that even if you have not had the actual experience of supervising, you have thought about it seriously and know how to talk about what you would do. If you have had supervisory experience, think about how you would answer questions like the following: Do you know the people you supervise? How? Do you ask them questions? About what? Do you compliment them? When? How? Do you reward them? When? How? When you are asked these or similar questions, place **special emphasis on motivation.** In fact, at least three-fourths of the time you spend answering leadership questions should be focused on how to motivate others.

Projecting Yourself As A Team Player

As Corporate America becomes more participative in its leadership style, as we de-emphasize titles, and as we look harder for those who can lead without being "the boss," we want people who can be team players. Simply stated, team players are individuals who have as much concern for their department's or company's success as for their own.

Being a team player is easier said than done. Some people find it impossible. While moving up the corporate ladder will always be important to people, a value for individual competitiveness should be subtle at best. Corporate America expects a philosophy that emphasizes helping others to be successful and to accomplish their corporate and personal goals.

I encourage you to examine your philosophy and determine whether you are known as a team player who works for the good of the team or as an individual who is more concerned about number one. If it's the latter, I recommend you take immediate steps to rethink the importance of being a team player.

Location Preference

What is your location preference? The answer to this question has probably caused more recruiters to get an instant bad attitude about an applicant than any other. The most frequent answer is, "I'm open," but "open" is **not** a definition of location. Recruiters don't believe it. **Don't use it.**

There are very few people in this world who are honestly open when it comes to a location preference, so answer this key question with a **regional** preference — the Northeast, the Midwest, the Southeast, etc. Don't give a city or a state; just specify a region. In difficult economic times, I recommend as broad a region as possible.

You may then want to follow the regional preference with a statement that you're open, saying, "I am not really looking for a location. I'm looking for a career. If everything is equal, then I would prefer the position to be in the Northeast. But, I have an enthusiastic attitude about going anywhere in the United States."

Be **smart**, as well as **honest**, in how you answer. If, for example, you're interviewing for a position in Cincinnati and your true preference is the Northeast, say your location preference would be east of the Mississippi River. That will include Cincinnati and the Northeast.

Never waste your time or a company's time by telling them something that is not true. If you're not willing to relocate, **then say so.** Analyze what you're willing to do. Be honest about it — with yourself and with interviewers. However, if you want a career with a Fortune 500 company, you must be willing to relocate. **Do not assume you can take the good and reject the bad.** When most companies are national/international and hiring individuals to become top managers, then it only makes sense that you will have to be willing to relocate.

Applicants sometimes say they have a great attitude about going anywhere in the United States with the exception of California and New York. I say to them that those are the two highest gross national product areas in the country. It doesn't make sense that you, as a development candidate, can eliminate the locations that produce the greatest dollar volume for your company. This doesn't mean you're going to have to live there your entire career, or even move to those states, but we can't assure you this won't happen. Applicants have also told me, "I want to live in the geographical area of my preference, and later I would be willing to move," or "I have been away at college and haven't been near my parents for four years. I want to go there to begin my career." We've heard these statements a million times. Once you are in the location of your choice, you won't have more reason to leave after two or three years; you will have more reason to stay. Corporations have had these experiences with employees and will not accept candidates' unwillingness to relocate.

If it is necessary for you to involve other people in your decision to relocate, do it early in your career search process. It is very unprofessional to decide you are not open for relocation after a company has spent time and money recruiting you. You should not work with a national recruiting firm if you have geographic restrictions. It is very disappointing to me to have applicants drop "surprises" on me after our firm has spent time and money on their behalf. It is discourteous and unfair for applicants to give recruiters the excuse that they didn't know their spouses, fiancés, or parents would react so negatively about their relocation.

On the other hand, we have a great attitude about putting you where you want to be, providing we have needs there, if we get a strong feeling that you are willing to accept any location. You must be honest not only with yourself but also with Corporate America. You must analyze exactly what it is that will allow you to accomplish the objectives you want and proceed to the type of company that allows you to accomplish those objectives. The time to think about this is before you interview, not afterwards.

(Dealing) With People

Thousands of applicants tell me they want a leadership role in Corporate America because they are very good at dealing with people. **Dealing** is a negative word. You deal with a problem. You do not deal with people. You work and interact with people. You deal with problems when required to do so. You may be very effective in dealing with problems, but a company is going to hire you because you are good at working with people.

"What Are Your Long- And Short-Term Career Goals?"

This question is frequently asked. While your answer is important, the delivery is equally important. **The question is really a communication question.** I have asked this question often, and I have yet to have anybody answer it properly. Did you notice there is no definition for long or short? Unless you describe what these two words mean to **you**, we can't evaluate your answer.

You might tell me that your short-term goal is to become familiar with your position, to get your feet on the ground, or to feel comfortable with what you're doing. If the recruiter's definition of short-term is two years, he will think you are pretty slow. You may think that two months is a good time period for a short-term goal. Do not answer the question until you give the recruiter your definition of long or short. Do **not** ask the recruiter for his definition. Provide your own.

Before you interview, think about your short-term goals. Write down at least five things you want to accomplish (both in your personal life and professional life) within the next year. Think about your long-term goals. Write down five things you want to accomplish within the next five to ten years.

Now, beginning with your short-term goals, outline how you plan to reach them. Break down each goal into intermediate steps which you can accomplish along the way. Establish a timeframe for the realistic accomplishment of each goal and use a calendar to remind yourself of each step to be taken. Do a similar, but broader, outline for your long-term goals. What short-term goals can you set to build toward reaching that long-term goal? Some goals may span 12 months, others several years. Think about how each goal fits into and affects the big picture of your life.

By doing this exercise, **you will discover how attainable your goals really are, and you will have a clear picture of your future achievements**. Whether in college or in business, you will find this to be rewarding and excellent preparation for attacking all projects and challenges.

Completing this exercise will help you identify and express the process you use to establish and attain goals and objectives when you interview. It will also provide you with examples of goals you have set and how you accomplished them.

It is important that you keep in mind how industry will analyze and judge your goals and accomplishments. Your goals and objectives should stretch you and "make you perspire" while reaching them. Industry feels the more **difficult** the objective, the more **significant** the achievement. You will need to prove to companies you have the ability to meet their expectations. Do this by giving them examples of goals and objectives you have set and met and yet did so by overcoming difficult obstacles.

"Why Should I Hire You?"
Let's say a company has a single opening and has interviewed three

or four candidates. They all look good. Then comes the question: Why should they hire you?

If you could get inside a recruiter's mind, he or she is really asking, "Why should I hire you **versus** the other candidates I'm considering?" The answer I get from applicants is almost always the same. "I'm the person who can get the job done. I have the credentials to do the job." That's what **everyone** says — and it really doesn't have **impact** or make an impression.

I am impressed with an applicant who says, "Mr. Cameron, I'm sure the kind of people you're interviewing all have good abilities. All of us are confident we can do the job. But, let me tell you about an asset that I feel is an integral part of me. You won't find anyone with a better **attitude.**"

This applicant explains it: "If I need to be here at 7 a.m. to get the job done, I'll be here. If I need to work through my lunch hour, I'll be here. If I need to work late, I'll be here. You don't have to worry about whether or not I'm going to be here — I **will be**. I'll be here with a positive attitude. Anytime you need anything done, give it to **me**. I'll get it done for you. That's what **separates me** from the other applicants." I honestly believe the **desire to apply one's ability** is more important than just **having** the ability.

You must answer the question, "Why should I hire you?" with words that have **unique** impact. Analyze yourself and determine the characteristics that set you apart from others. This is not the time to copy an answer. It must accurately describe **you**. Obviously, if this company hires you, they will be looking for you to use this inner characteristic in your day-to-day job performance.

When you answer the question, don't ramble. You'll become boring and lose the recruiter. I recall an applicant of mine who was being interviewed by a major company. He'd been asked six times why he wanted sales and six times he tried to explain. He could have made real impact by using fewer words, such as: "I am **going** to have a career in sales. While I'd like to have the opportunity to have the sales position with your company, I want to assure you, I **will** have it with some high-quality company."

This example is similar to a situation of a young woman who tried to explain why a job wasn't done right. The more she talked, the more guilty she sounded. She could have said simply, "I didn't accomplish the objective. I understand what I did wrong. It won't happen again."

Don't explain and continue to explain. It's so much easier to make an impact with a **few** words versus **many**. And, remember, when you're asked why you want a career in Corporate America, be emphatic. Give proof. Put credibility in your answer.

I like to hear an applicant say, "Roger, I **am** going to have a career in Corporate America." I rarely hear words like these. Answer questions with impact based on the solid research and clear thinking you've done. You've reached a conclusion and can verbalize it. Remember, you must back up your rhetoric with **proof and evidence**.

The Negative Interview
The negative interview is designed to test your conviction about your career objective. Companies are looking for people with conviction. They use interviewing techniques to determine whether applicants have the necessary determination and conviction. If they can talk you out of what you say you want to do, then they have proven you have too little conviction. Particularly in the area of manufacturing, you might be asked, "What is your opinion of shift work?" The reason for the question is that people leave manufacturing in Corporate America because they don't like shift work. It's difficult to say in an interview, "I'm really excited about

shift work," but one of your early promotion levels in manufacturing is to manage a 24-hour operation. Different shift times create unique problems. Managers have their own idiosyncrasies in motivating subordinates to perform, so if you know one of your early lines of promotion is to manage a 24-hour operation, then, obviously, it would be better to have experienced those different shifts yourself. Also, many of you will want to get your MBA or MS in a technical field. Many times, you can get a better quality master's degree during daytime hours than in the evening. Sometimes, going on shifts early in your career is an ideal time for you to work toward your master's degree.

When recruiters attempt to talk you out of a job, they may use different negative interview tactics, such as, "Well, you're an outstanding candidate, and I really feel our company should hire you. However, I feel you would be better suited for position **A** than the position you are interviewing for." You've got to challenge them. They're simply testing your ability to be committed and convinced about the position. If you are applying for a sales position, the recruiters may say something similar to this: "Sales — I think you have strong poise and self-confidence, but you have to understand that with sales negative situations are going to occur within a day. Someone may slam the door on you or cancel an appointment at the last minute. You're going to waste some time in a day. It's very difficult for you to get organized and to effectively manage your time. You have the opportunity to select other very outstanding positions in our company." Again, they are simply attempting to determine your conviction. Be careful! Properly used, the "negative" interview can be a very useful tool in determining an applicant's ability to handle adverse situations. I myself do it when I have some doubt about whether the applicant is right for the job.

In the follow-up interviewing process, a couple of companies have a designated negative interviewer whose sole purpose is to try to talk applicants out of the job they're seeking. Some of the applicants I have sent to these companies have not listened to me, and they have allowed themselves to be talked out of a job. I've actually had applicants come back to me and say, "Roger, I remember what you said, but I'm confident that's not what the company was doing. They actually thought I was better for something else." I moaned when I heard this. Then, true enough (as I get feedback), they'd been ruled out for lack of conviction. You **must** have conviction. You **must** know what you want. You **must** be able to focus and concentrate on that objective. Don't let anybody sway you.

Occasionally, the negative interview is used to determine poise and self-confidence. Sometimes, recruiters use it "to push on the end of your nose" to see what reaction they will get. While this is rarely used in interviewing today, I want to make you aware of it. Normally, the type of negative questions you will hear will be, " A 3.5 grade point average — why wasn't it better?" or "I see your spouse bought you a tie and you have to wear it." First of all, you will usually find the recruiter will ask a negative question on a **positive** point. In other words, it isn't for the purpose of embarrassing an applicant. It is for the purpose of determining how you handle a negative situation. In Corporate America, you will not always be in a positive situation. There will be times you'll be in combative meetings. You will have to defend your viewpoint. Recruiters want to see if you have gained the maturity and poise to be able to do so in a positive manner. Do your neck and ears turn red? Do you put on the boxing gloves, or do you simply square your shoulders, look the recruiter in the eye, and handle it positively? It may come up in interviews. Always remember, the recruiter's objective is not to embarrass but to establish conviction, poise, and self-confidence. Be determined to show that you do.

Behavioral Traits
The behavioral interview is being used more and more and is an effective tool for evaluation. The goal of the interview is to uncover

the applicant's behavioral traits, those skills or characteristics that the applicant applies consciously or unconsciously to accomplish objectives. **(Do not attempt to go through this exercise until you have completed your work in Chapter 4 in Objective/Subjective Assets.)** Some companies refer to this interview as the "basic characteristics interview"; others call it the "competency-based" interview. In this interview the recruiter listens to your illustrations of previous experiences to identify characteristics integral to a successful development candidate.

Most companies have determined the behavioral traits that they consider a successful employee must possess. Not surprisingly, companies' lists are very similar.

Today, it's taboo for you to actually state the trait. You can't say, for example, that you're "intelligent and competitive." As I have previously stated, you must illustrate these characteristics verbally by discussing your past accomplishments.

How will you know in an interview when a recruiter is looking for **your** behavioral traits? The recruiter will ask you **how** you did something. Anytime you hear a recruiter ask "How?" let it be a signal to you that you need to give examples of your competencies used in accomplishing goals or the problem resolution. The recruiter might say, "Tell me about an accomplishment and **how** you achieved it," or "Tell me about a problem you encountered and **how** you solved it."

To prepare for the behavioral interview, start by finding a quiet spot and analyzing exactly **how you** accomplish difficult objectives. This isn't a five-minute job. I envision it taking you a full day — or even more. As you examine your past accomplishments, make a list of those **common** behavioral traits (competencies, characteristics) that appear in situation after situation. Note how some traits are automatic, or subconscious, and how others require a conscious effort on your part. List the traits that appear frequently and cause outstanding performance. This is a key point. The trait should be developed to a level that results in exceptional achievement; otherwise, the list is meaningless to you. We all organize, manage our time, and interact with others, but do we do it to the degree that we would be considered outstanding in each trait?

Next, I would suggest you prioritize your list of traits and keep them firmly in mind with examples of accomplishments. As a result, in an interview you'll be armed with the information about your most outstanding traits so you can give the recruiter a concise, articulate description.

Try this exercise to help you identify the traits you possess that you feel are most noteworthy. Lean back in your chair, close your eyes, and visualize an individual who has worked with you or for you and whose performance was outstanding. Think about what you most admired about that individual's performance. I have asked applicants to do this in interviews, and they have consistently mentioned the same characteristics. The individual they describe is always a hard worker, has a positive attitude, is goal-oriented, and is a team player. Now, think about the traits you have identified and which of those you think would describe you as well. Think about situations that have occurred in which you have used these outstanding traits and accomplished your goals to an exceptional degree. Use the tape recorder to record your answer to a recruiter.

Another exercise that may help you determine your personal traits is to pick up the phone and pretend you are calling Roger Cameron at Cameron-Brooks, Professional Recruiting Firm, to have me recruit development candidates for you. Describe for me the behavioral traits you expect these individuals to possess. Again, you will see recruiter after recruiter asking for similar competencies.

Additionally, Appendix C contains a list of behavioral traits. Use this list to help you identify those characteristics you think best describe your strengths.

The following are types of characteristics recruiters want to see in a behavioral answer:
- Goal orientation, success-driven, make-it-happen attitude
- Effective use of time
- Interaction with peers, superiors, and subordinates
- Organizational ability
- Prioritization
- Pre-problem solution ability
- Creativeness
- Innovativeness
- Competitiveness
- Sense of urgency
- Effective communication
- Team player mentality
- Technical competency
- Work ethic

Record your significant accomplishments or problems solved on tape, and then listen to your answers. Remember, we're **not** looking for you to say, "I was goal-oriented. I effectively used my time." We need to hear a description of the action you took to see how you resolve a problem and accomplish an objective.

The behavioral traits interview is being used more and more and is considered one of the finest interviews given. Recruiters know the specific traits they are looking for. Be certain to prepare well for the interview. You can't count on the answers coming naturally. If they don't come out of your tape recorder, they're not going to come out of your mouth in an interview.

STOP!
DON'T READ FURTHER UNTIL YOU HAVE
RECORDED SIGNIFICANT ACCOMPLISHMENTS
AND ANALYZED YOUR ANSWERS.

See Appendix D for an Interview Self-Evaluation Sheet you can use to evaluate your performance after each interview.

CHAPTER 8

"As an Admissions Officer at the Air Force Academy, I am always frustrated when I find a student with tremendous potential who has wasted the chance to prepare for challenging college and career options. It saddens me when these students are too short-sighted to realize that hard work now almost always pays off big in the future. Roger Cameron knows what it takes to develop the skills and backgrounds that employers want. Learn from him — pay the price now, and you won't be disappointed."

> — Cpt. Leon Lowman
> Assistant Chief Minority Enrollment
> United States Air Force Academy

CHAPTER 8

Consider The Reasons For Rejection

The following are actual comments from interviewers describing applicants who were declined. You will notice that some of the points are similar, but these similarities only emphasize their importance. The comments are grouped under four categories: preparation, communication, energy level, and leadership qualities. After reading four or five comments, it might be easy for you to say, "Oh, that's not me" or "I've learned enough." Please, do yourself a favor and read them all.

Preparation

- **Lacked conviction; was difficult to hear.** So often recruiters say, "Roger, I like everything the applicant said, but I'm not convinced that he meant what he said." Sometimes we have applicants tell us they have consistently been soft-spoken. Their parents and teachers have often asked them to speak up, but they feel that it is natural for them to speak softly and that there is nothing they can do about it. *I have found it helpful for applicants to use a tape recorder to correct this problem. Place the recorder across the room from you, and then project your voice into it without yelling. Do this for an hour every day. You may read from a book or pick a subject and spontaneously give a speech on it. The point is to project your voice. Don't cheat. Don't place the microphone so it is easier for the recorder to pick up the sound. Buy an inexpensive tape recorder rather than the best machine. The key is not to get a recorder that will pick up a weak voice. The test is to project your voice so that soon it will become natural for you to speak in a forceful, convincing manner.*

You do not have to be soft-spoken for the rest of your life. I am not suggesting that you transform from someone who is mild-mannered and soft-spoken into someone who is loud and obnoxious. I am talking about presenting yourself in a professional and convincing manner. Watch people you know — for example, some of your professors and other students who have voices to which you respond positively — and watch how they project. Listen to the tone and volume of their voices. If you determine after working on this independently for several weeks or months, that this isn't doing the job, then don't be afraid to go for outside help. Go to a diction instructor — someone who can help you use your voice in a better manner — or take a speech course. Do not accept failure in increasing the power and the impact of your voice.

- **Well rehearsed, but not specific when probed.** The applicant talked in generalizations. For example, to the question, "How did you build teamwork?" he answered, "I build teamwork with my subordinates." This generalization is not acceptable to recruiters. The applicant should have given specific examples of **how** he built teamwork. *Be sure to do your homework so that you can give specifics and evidence in answer to questions.*

- **Too rehearsed — said what the recruiter wanted to hear.** The applicant showed by his answers that he was not a confident person. Recruiters are sharp. They will see right through a facade. *Prepare. Don't give someone else's answers or deliver by rote. It will not work. You must prepare in advance to be yourself and to convince the recruiter that you are the right person for the job.*

- **Couldn't articulate and give specific examples of accomplishments.** Had the applicant used her tape recorder before the interview and listened to herself, this probably would not have happened. *You cannot be successful as a development* *candidate without quality preparation. No one can speak in a concise, articulate manner without hard work and preparation.*

- **Textbook answers.** The applicant might have felt that by giving perfect answers, the recruiter would think he was perfect. *If you're not comfortable enough or not prepared enough to be relaxed and be your smart self, the recruiter will see right through you. Would you bring someone into your company who you felt lacked confidence or, in fact, was a fake?*

- **Bad questions.** This applicant showed lack of understanding of the position and career. *If you've spent the necessary time to get information about the job and company, you'll be able to do some pre-work. Write out your questions before you interview and practice verbalizing them. During your interview listen carefully to the recruiter so you will be able to formulate appropriate questions.*

- **Programmed answers.** Some applicants give answers that appear canned, even shallow. They need to recognize the importance of sincerity in their delivery. *Do your homework so you can digest the information and deliver it in your own personal style.*

- **Superficial answers.** The applicant gave answers indicating lack of depth, quality, self-insight, and comprehension. *Be aware that recruiters are looking for these characteristics. They are the foundation of a development candidate.*

- **Same questions as everyone else.** The applicant did not listen carefully and did not gather sufficient information to ask specific, relevant questions. *You cannot ask generic questions. Your questions must be relevant to that company and that position. They must have a purpose.*

- **No competencies.** The applicant didn't listen, understand, or comprehend the competency-based interview. *You must verbally illustrate your key characteristics without naming them. This is not easy, but you must find the time to prepare for this most frequent interview.*

- **Could not relate background.** The applicant couldn't draw parallels from past performance. *Be sure to study the position for which you are applying before you interview so that you are prepared to relate how your experience and skills can be applied to the job.*

- **Was not flexible about location.** The applicant took one second to say he was open, but he then spent five minutes talking about why he had a preference. This contradiction made the recruiter question the applicant's believability. *While being flexible about location may be difficult for you, it is important for you to be certain about your willingness to relocate. Be sure you have a positive, concise way to describe your position and stick to it. You appear to be indecisive otherwise.*

- **Didn't know what she wanted to do.** The applicant didn't prepare for the interview by analyzing her knowledge, skills, achievements and objective/subjective assets. She lacked quality self-insight. She may have thought she could wing it and talk off the top of her head. *Be sure you do whatever it takes before the interview to know specifically how your achievements and skills relate to the career you are seeking. Employers want to know how you can contribute to their success, so be ready to tell them.*

Communication
- **Rambled. Poor communicator.** The applicant tried to tell the recruiter too much. He ran out of time and appeared unfocused. *You can decrease the chance that you will ramble when answering questions by spending quality time before the interview thinking*

about some typical questions that may be asked and how you can answer concisely. When you are asked a question during the interview, take a few seconds to organize your thoughts. Answer succinctly, but be careful not to give answers that are so abbreviated they have no substance.

- **Talked nonstop. Didn't listen and didn't relate the background.** The applicant didn't look for cues from the recruiter about how the delivery of his answers was being accepted. *Be sensitive to the recruiter and listen to what he says so you can relate your background to the job and company requirements. To be a development candidate, you must actively reflect, organize, deliver, and then be quiet. Almost 75 percent of an executive's time is spent listening, so you want to be sure you exhibit this characteristic in the interview.*

- **Too much slang.** The applicant didn't realize that using informal language is not acceptable in a job interview. Recruiters are turned off by slang or repeated words, such as "O.K.," "roger," "do you know what I mean," or "you know." *Omit slang or repetitious words from your conversation.*

- **Couldn't get anything out of her.** This applicant had difficulty discussing her background and qualifications in a pleasant, conversational style. *You must relax in an interview and help the recruiter know the real you. To prepare for a discussion of your qualifications, write down the significant achievements you have made that point to relevant skills the position would require, and then practice verbalizing them. Next, practice "interviewing" with a friend indicating you want the "interview" to be relaxed. Ask your friend to help you achieve this goal by giving you suggestions. The point is not to memorize a canned speech but to be familiar with major points you will want to make in the interview so you are not caught off guard with nothing to say. A recruiter will not **pull** information from you.*

- **Not an open communicator.** The applicant was guarded in his manner and had trouble revealing his true self. *If you have prepared adequately for your interview and have practiced with another person, you will have taken a big step in being able to talk openly with the interviewer.*

- **Lectured.** The applicant didn't display a natural, easy-going communication style. *You must speak with, not to, the interviewer. Strive to listen to the interviewer and to answer questions as succinctly as possible so you don't appear to be lecturing.*

- **Didn't answer precise questions.** The applicant's rambling answer indicated he may not have listened to everything the recruiter stated in his question. *You must actively listen to every word before answering a question and take the time to formulate a direct answer.*

- **Overused first names.** The applicant called the interviewer by name too many times during the interview in an effort to establish a comfortable rapport. *Names must be used in moderation. Calling someone by name three or four times during a forty-five minute interview is appropriate. It is also important to deliver the interviewer's name in a sincere and natural way.*

- **Poor eye contact.** By not maintaining eye contact with the interviewer, the applicant gave the impression that he had low self-esteem and was lacking in self-confidence. *Be sure to do what it takes to establish and maintain eye contact with other individuals before you interview.*

Energy Level
- **Didn't show interest.** The applicant had poor posture and slumped in her chair. She also showed very little enthusiasm in

either her voice quality or the statements she made. *Recruiters are looking for candidates who exhibit energy and enthusiasm for the job. Be prepared to convince them you are just such a person.*

- **Not natural; too stiff.** The applicant was unable to relax and be natural. *You should be able to carry on a two-way conversation in an easy, natural, and enthusiastic manner.*

- **Obnoxious.** The applicant was overly aggressive. *While it is important to be enthusiastic, it is also necessary to observe how the recruiter is reacting to your delivery. Be sensitive to any tell-tale signs of adverse reaction and adjust. Practice with others before you interview and get feedback about your style.*

- **Reserved; low energy level.** This applicant may not have known the importance of selling himself. He needed to show his ability to handle many tasks which can only be done with lots of energy. *To make a recruiter believe you can handle a job, you must be excited about the opportunity. You must show enthusiasm and a high energy level. It makes no difference whether you are applying for a position in engineering, production planning, or finance. You are first and foremost a development candidate. You must project an image similar to that of the top 10 percent of all managers. As a leader your attitude is contagious. Would you allow your team to be slow? Unenthusiastic? Bored? Not sharp? You must show your enthusiasm and prove you can go the extra mile.*

- **Too intense.** The applicant was too uptight. He was not relaxed. *Companies want professional, poised people. Whether you are in a sales or leadership role, people will respond better if you are relaxed. You must always be comfortable with a pleasant, professional sense of humor.*

Leadership Qualities

- **Not a team player.** The applicant impressed the recruiter as being too authoritative. *Companies demand a leader who can be a team captain rather than a dominating coach. Recruiters are looking for candidates who will be able to motivate workers by getting their trust versus being their boss. When you practice for the interview, write down examples of how you have been a team player in any of your school or work experiences. Refer to how you delegated authority and encouraged participation and why others responded to your style. Then, practice presenting these experiences out loud.*

- **Good supervision, but limited success.** This applicant had responsibility relating to leadership but could not articulate how he had positively carried out his responsibilities and had an impact on his team. *Be prepared in the interview to discuss how your actions as a leader caused positive change and motivated your team to significant accomplishments.*

- **No initiative. Simply a caretaker.** In a fast-paced environment of highly skilled workers, you must creatively solve problems on your own initiative. This individual seemed content with the status quo. *It is easier to go through life as a follower. This is not what we're looking for in a development candidate. You must have the initiative to enhance performance without prompting from your superiors.*

- **Unrealistic regarding promotion.** The applicant stated a requirement for promotion within the first six months. *Nothing will scare away companies faster than for you to make unreasonable demands. It is important to be ambitious but realistic. You must temper your expectations. There are many factors that must be considered for promotion. You will not be promoted overnight. Be realistic in self-evaluation and about* *promotion opportunity relative to your abilities. Unrealistic expectations usually mean a person expects too much too soon. It is a hard, long road to the top. To reach the top, the road must be filled with significant contribution.*

I have given you the most prevalent reasons recruiters have ruled out particular applicants over the years. As you look at these reasons, note that you have total control over most of them. It's a matter of speaking up with enthusiasm, listening actively, addressing the questions directly, giving substance to your answers, having accurate self-insight, and being concise in what you have to say. I would encourage you to study this section very carefully before going into any interview and to remind yourself of these factors just prior to the interview itself.

CHAPTER 9

"Roger Cameron knows what U.S. industry needs. He taught me simple techniques to make me stand out as a person employers would seek. I used his guidance in job interviews, and suddenly I had more offers for high paying, challenging jobs than I ever expected."

— Anita Riddle
  Environmental Engineer
  Mobil Oil Corporation

Move Toward The Job Offer

Dollars and Sense

When you're talking with a company and they ask what salary you expect, don't tell them that you're open. You know you're not open. Every time applicants say that to me, I say, "Fine, we'll pay you $18,000." Suddenly, they're backpedaling. "Well, that's not reasonable." I reply, "It isn't reasonable that you tell me you're open."

So, how can you handle this question of money? I recommend that you say something similar to this: "Money is important to me. I want to get what I'm worth, but it's only one of many factors I'll be considering. I'm not going to take a job based solely on money. I'm going to take a job based on the quality of the company, the quality of the career path, the operating philosophy of the company, the location, benefits, travel, etc." Analyze those factors that are specifically important to you before answering this question.

I recommend giving a salary range of no more than $2,000 to $3,000 (between suggested salaries). Recruiters are not going to accept a $10,000 range (for example, $30,000 to $40,000).

In the hiring process, you're going to be paid on the basis of credentials. Research the marketplace. Determine what your value is to Corporate America. Set a fair market value — one with which you and Corporate America can live. Your college placement center should be able to give you accurate salary expectations. When you are given a salary range, be realistic and measure your

overall skills, experience, and performance relative to your peers. Do you deserve the top of the range?

Pay Raises
There are three ways you can get increased compensation in Corporate America.

- **Annual pay raise:** This raise is just what it says. It is granted annually. There is no specific formula as to how much you can expect in a year. Companies have a general formula based on objective performance factors.

- **Promotional pay raise:** With a grade level or position level promotion, you will usually receive a pay raise.

- **Merit pay raise:** Merit pay raise is given for performance above the expected norms. This is not easy to obtain when you are performing among other outstanding employees. It is for exceptional, high achievement.

In your first year in Corporate America, it would be unlikely for you to receive more than an annual increase. But, in your second year, it would not be unusual for you to receive one or more of the three increases in compensation. Again, remember, you will be paid and promoted according to your performance. There are factors in addition to your performance that will be considered — for instance, the overall performance of your company. If your individual performance does not have an impact on the company's bottom line, it **could** have an impact on your pay raises.

Being a typical American, you'll never be paid what you feel you're worth. I know individuals in industry who are paid $300,000 a year, and they still feel they are underpaid. That doesn't mean they don't wear a smile every day. It's just what human nature is all about. There is never an ideal world. You don't see outstanding performers at Mobil, IBM, Procter & Gamble, and DuPont leaving because of dissatisfaction with compensation and benefits. Corporate America takes very good care of its people. You earn it first; then, it's given to you. You won't get it before you go out and earn it.

Transitional Concerns
Students often have concern about the physical transition itself. You are going to find that your company will virtually walk you through each step. Normal procedures include an expense paid trip for both the new employee and spouse (if married) to the location of the new position so housing accommodations can be found. While all companies are different, generally speaking, you will also be given guidance on realtors, financial institutions, and neighborhoods. And, of course, all normal expenses will be paid. Always **remember**, each company has its own policies, and before you create an expenditure, you should determine if it is reimbursable. Also, companies normally cover all expenses, including moving furniture and car mileage. Applicants have been extremely pleased with the relocation benefits they have received. Corporations know that relocations can cause frustration and unwanted anxieties which they work hard to eliminate.

We encourage you to talk with other students who have already interviewed and accepted positions. It can be comforting to speak with someone who has actually been "in your shoes."

$3,000 Is A Crucial Figure
Companies spend approximately $3,000 on a follow-up interview to cover airline tickets, rental cars, taxis, hotels, food, and managers' time.

Not unlike applicants, recruiters are selfish. They are most concerned, and rightly so, about their own careers. Frequently, recruiters are young people who are willing to sit through numerous interviews. But, they're aware that every time they say "yes" to a follow-up interview, they have, in fact, signed a company check for $3,000.

They're aware they can't sign too many of these checks and then have applicants declined by upper management. Their record will begin to reflect on their credibility. Too many applicants are simply unaware of the recruiter's situation. You must help the recruiter feel good about spending $3,000 for the follow-up. You can do that by giving the best possible interview.

On this dollar amount basis alone, many recruiters will eliminate an applicant. Today, many companies are sending two or more recruiters to interview at career conferences. They feel it is less expensive to get a second and even a third opinion at these conferences. Then, when applicants are given follow-up interviews, they are more assured the rest of the managers will agree with their opinions. It's a better decision and less costly to get multiple judgments at the conference before flying an applicant for a follow-up interview. Also, it assures a higher rate of offer to follow-up ratio.

We're finding companies are increasingly aware of recruiting costs. **Therefore, remember that $3,000 the next time you step in front of a recruiter.**

What Is Your Definition Of A Job Offer?

You are not assured a job offer simply because a recruiter smiles, requests a follow-up interview, shows interest, says he'll get back in touch, or he tells you he likes your background.

Applicants frequently define an offer as money, benefits, location, or the position. These are **components** of an offer — but still not the clear, succinct definition. An offer occurs when the **control switches hands** — when it goes from the company to you, the individual.

Prior to this point, the company is in control and can say yes or no, but **you** can't do anything. The first time you're in control is when you have the offer. At this point, you have the ability to say yes or no to the company. That's the bottom-line definition of an offer.

A lot can happen between a recruiter's smile and the actual offer. Companies sometimes interview an applicant eight or nine times and still do not offer the position. Sometimes, an applicant is told he/she will receive an offer and then the company fills the position with someone else or has to remove the position from the marketplace because of economics. Therefore, you should never think you have an offer until it is, in fact, in your pocket — when **you** can say yes or no.

There's a difference between the pursuit and the offer. For example, if you know that to get an offer for a certain position requires five to seven interviews, you can consider the first three to five interviews "pursuit." If you've reached the last phases of the interview process, tell the company you are interested in an offer, rather than simply pursuit, and use an upbeat close as mentioned on page 140. You might say, "I want to reiterate my very strong interest in this position. I want you to know that I would like to receive an offer." You must decide, at this point, if you want to receive an offer so you can evaluate it **in relation to other offers,** or if, in fact, this is **the** job you want to accept.

If it's the latter, then say, "I want to tell you that my strong interest in this position is because of your company and the quality of people." (Remember, use specifics relevant to that company.) "I would like you to know I want an offer so I can accept it." **But, never cross that line unless you truly know this is the job you want.**

Accepting A Career Position
This is one of the most critical moments. When you accept a position, do so with a primary person — the individual for whom you would be working or the person who made the offer. **Always**

accept prior to deadline — never ever wait until the deadline. If you do, the company doesn't know if you're accepting because time has run out or because you want the job.

Be extremely upbeat in accepting. For instance, you might say, "I just have to tell you that I don't need any more time to determine that I want to have my career with your company. I want you to know I'm extremely excited about getting started. What is my next step?" And the company will go through the upcoming procedures with you.

I always tell about Janis who now works for me. Originally, we interviewed her several times. While on a recruiting trip, I called in and learned Janis had accepted. "Is she excited?" I asked an associate. "Well, really, I don't know," I was told. "She said, 'Well, I **guess** I'll take your job.'" I was concerned about her lack of enthusiasm for the job, and I even suggested we call her back and withdraw our offer. Fortunately, we didn't. Janis has been with us since 1985 and is an integral part of our organization. I wouldn't know what to do without her. But, I'll never forget her acceptance, and I've kidded her about it over the years.

Once you've accepted an offer, you should write a letter to everyone with whom you made contact at that company. Thank them for their part — for showing you the manufacturing facility, spending a day with you in the field, or giving you insight into company operations. It would be a shame if you went to work for the company and met one of the above individuals in the hall, and he or she didn't know you were with the firm. This is where your professional attitude in **developing relationships** should begin. It's probably one of the most critical steps in starting a company career.

Declining An Offer

When you decline an offer, be sure to be professional and courteous. The minute you know you are not going to accept a company's offer, telephone and let them know. It is best not to send a letter because it will take two or three days for the company to receive it. Be conscious of the fact that once an offer goes out for a position, all recruiting for that position must stop. The company may have other people in the recruiting process waiting to hear from them about the position you are going to decline. The longer those people wait without being pursued, the less interest they have in that company and the higher the probability they will be hired by another company. **Therefore, never hold an offer when you know you're not going to accept the position.**

Be honest and candid with the company when you decline the offer. First of all, tell them which company you will be working for. You're developing relationships in Corporate America. Let them know. Many times, it is best just to say, "This was one of the most difficult decisions I've ever had to make in my life, but I have made the decision to go to Company A. What I'll be doing with that company is going into (name of position). I just have to tell you the two locations were very similar, the money was very similar. I was very excited about what I saw in your company. It's just that I felt a bit more compatibility with the other firm. I don't know if I can tell you what it was. I just felt a little more comfortable in the other company's environment."

When you inform the company you are declining the position you have accepted, **never** tell them it was because of location. Remember that the company spent $3,000 to fly you in for follow-up interviews. You led them to believe the location was totally acceptable to you, so for you to later decline because of location is to say you were dishonest and lacked professionalism. The road of life has many curves. You never know when you're going to veer back and run into that person, situation, and company again. If you accept a position with another company because the location is more acceptable to you, you might say, "I was sincerely open for your location. I had a preference which I pointed out in the interview. The other company offered my location preference. It was the only factor that tipped the offer in their favor. It wasn't that your location wasn't acceptable to me. It was just that the other offer was more acceptable."

It is also a good idea to follow up your decline with a professional letter of thanks for all the costs the company might have incurred for your follow-up interviews and the time their managers took with you. Tell them you will refer their company to other students who are graduating. **Never burn a bridge.** You never know when you may want to walk over it again.

Working With Women

If you are a male student, it is important to recruiters to determine whether you have a positive attitude about working with women. There are those who give us the perception that they have incorrect ideas about women's roles in business. Sometimes their opinions are expressed in ways that lead us to believe they won't have good working relationships with women as peers or superiors. Frequently, applicants have said they spoke with one of my secretaries. When I've questioned them about whether this person said she was a secretary, they have indicated they assumed the woman was a secretary because she answered the phone.

I can relate a story which is an excellent example of this poor attitude. A recruiter called an applicant and asked him to call a woman in his office to get the details of an offer. When the applicant had received the information, he was to call the recruiter back. The applicant did as instructed and called the recruiter and said, "I called your secretary and got all the details." The recruiter then asked the applicant if the woman had identified herself as his secretary, and the applicant admitted he had just assumed she was a secretary. On the basis of this incident, the recruiter felt the applicant was biased and withdrew the job offer.

Instead of assuming the woman with whom he spoke was a secretary, the applicant could have referred to her position in a generic way. He could have said, "I spoke with your associate." In this way he would not have labeled her with a certain position.

I encourage you to think seriously about the roles of women and men in business. If working with women is below you or you feel women don't have the ability to compete with you, then don't apply for a position in Corporate America.

Minority Hiring/Managing Diversity

I have lived through the days when recruiting minorities was mandated by government. Major corporations were given quotas. Companies hired and promoted for the wrong reasons. I watched companies promote for the wrong reasons. There were many times when I shook my head and thought how difficult it was to be a minority seeking employment in U.S. corporations.

Circumstances have changed over the years. They haven't changed as fast as I feel they should have, nor as fast as many minorities think they should have. However, I can honestly say that, today, most of our top companies in Corporate America are colorblind. These companies have developed excellent programs to monitor minority growth. I feel a sense of personal gratification that I helped place many minority applicants in top leadership positions in Corporate America. Is it a perfect world? It is not. However, I do think the new theory of "managing diversity" is headed in the right direction.

In many companies today, when two people are competing for a job and have equal qualifications, the minority will get the nod for promotion. Minorities should receive this consideration until we get a better balance in Corporate America among minority and non-minority groups. I've always felt it was important to be candid and outspoken when discussing issues with different minority groups.

I think it is extremely important that you are hired for the right reason — performance — and not because you are a minority. While you may receive some initial reward if you are hired as a minority, it is not the way to establish a career. One should build only on the basis of performance.

As the year 2000 approaches, demographics in the U.S. will change dramatically.

- Women will account for 47 percent of the workforce.
- Sixty-one percent of all women will be employed.
- White men will account for less than 40 percent of the total U.S. labor force.

By the year 2010:

- The U.S. population is expected to grow by 42 million.
- Hispanics will account for 47 percent of the growth.
- Blacks will account for 22 percent.
- Asians and other people of color will account for 18 percent.
- Whites will account for 13 percent.

(Statistics are from the U.S. Census Bureau as reported in *USA Today*, 8/26/91.)

Managers must demonstrate the ability to manage this workforce of great diversity of backgrounds, lifestyles, values, and opinions. The "typical" employee is changing and will continue to change. U.S. corporations are challenged by the extraordinary competitive pressures in the world today. To be competitive domestically and globally will be impossible if the talents of all employees are not developed for maximum productivity. Therefore, managers will be measured by their ability to manage this diversity.

As you prepare for your interviews, be aware that you will be scrutinized for your attitudes regarding others with backgrounds different from yours. Recognize that recruiters will be looking for people who are non-judgmental, who consider others' opinions before making decisions, who value people with different backgrounds and values, and who seek to understand and accept them.

CHAPTER 10

"The purpose of education is not knowledge, but ACTION! Having successfully recruited and prepared thousands of top candidates for the FORTUNE 500, Roger Cameron is highly qualified to give practical, action-oriented ideas on how college students need to prepare to go to work for the best companies in America. Read *Your Career Fast Track*! But, more importantly, take action and DO what Roger recommends."

—Walter Hailey, Founder
Planned Marketing Associates, Inc.

CHAPTER 10 ═══════════════

Meet The Challenges Of The Future

Every day, companies send out recruiters with more unique and difficult positions to fill. As a result, the college student needs to be even better qualified. As companies become more "high tech" and thoroughly computer-based, we have a wider range of positions and career paths.

Recruiters look for candidates with "BLT" — **believability, likability, and trust.** We want wholesome people who respect individual qualities but don't have to brag about them, who are tough but not obnoxious, who are intelligent but can work with both the intellectual and non-intellectual, and, most of all, who know how to **make it happen,** the bottom line of development candidates.

These applicants can accomplish tough, demanding objectives. They don't give excuses. Excuses are so easy to find, much easier than reaching down deep in one's self to go that extra mile.

Day One Of Your Career

Be prepared for your first day on the job. As soon as you accept an offer, head for the library and thoroughly study your chosen industry. Call your new employer and ask for a recommendation for a course of study, books to read, and actions to take before starting to work. Not only will this impress your new employer, but it will help you to be as knowledgeable as you can be when you begin. Show your organizational ability by having your organizer open and on your desk within minutes of starting work.

Leave college behind you. Some offices I visit are decorated with college caps, banners, pictures, cups, ash trays, etc. It's fine to be proud of your alma mater, but try being a little more subtle about it. As a new recruit to the workforce, people may think of you as young and fresh out of school. Placing a lot of school mementos in your office will just emphasize this fact. Choose objects for your office that represent what you are doing today.

Being Professional

One definition of a **professional is this: a person who does what's expected of him/her — always.** This isn't an outlook that's selectively applied. It's a lifestyle. No person can be highly successful without applying it on a full-time basis. In my career I have seen many professional people who have gone up the corporate ladder very rapidly. These people are extremely reliable. When they tell you they will do something, you can count on them to do it. **If you are sincerely determined to be a success in Corporate America, do what you say you're going to do. Do what's expected of you at all times, not just when it's convenient.**

Recognizing People As Individuals

Learn to use first names. It's important. I remember interviewing an individual in Clarksville, Tennessee. I'd been at a hotel there for three days. With me was a new, young recruiter who was having a hard time using first names.

The day we left, I told Betty (the waitress we usually saw in the hotel restaurant) that we were leaving. She burst into tears. Both the other recruiter and I were very surprised.

Then she explained, "Mr. Cameron, I have to tell you how much enjoyment you've given me this week. I wear this name tag, but nobody ever calls me by my first name. Instead, it's, 'Hey, waitress,' 'Hey, you,' 'Ma'am,' or 'Miss.' What a pleasure to have someone recognize me as an individual." When she left, I saw that my associate was moved. And I've never known him **not** to use first names since that experience.

Whether it's your gardener, a housekeeper, or the person filling your gas tank, **treat them as individuals.** Don't make them feel they're there simply to serve you. It will make **you** feel better, and I promise you it will make **them** feel better, too. If they're not wearing name tags, ask them their names. I've never had people insulted because I've asked, but I can't count the times they showed surprise — almost shock — that I cared enough to ask, and then actually used their names. It's nice to be important, but it's more important to be nice.

Corporate America today is a participative work environment. If you don't have the ability to work with a diverse group of people and if you don't have the ability to show you are a people person, you frankly don't belong in Corporate America. The Fortune 500 are the very best companies, and they are fanatically participative.

One of my top companies says, "If an individual doesn't have the innate ability to come to work in the morning and say good morning to the janitor, he or she is not the kind of person we want working for our company." You must recognize people as individuals who are worthy of your respect.

One of the most gratifying letters I've ever received was from an applicant I had placed with Mobil Chemical, a division of Mobil Oil. I will never forget it. He was very happy that he had chosen a great career field and had landed a job with a great company. He realized that his corporate career was now essentially made with good performance. He said the thing he really gained from us was the understanding of the importance of using people's first names. He went on to state how proud he was that he knew the first names of the people who put gas in his car, who did his laundry, and who waited on him in restaurants. Today, he never fails to look immediately at someone's name tag and use their first name two or three times. I guess I was as proud of receiving that letter as he was of learning the importance of using first names.

Please don't come to us with this excuse: "Roger, it's very difficult for me. I used 'sir' and 'ma'am' all the way through junior high, high school, and college." We say to you, "That's fine, but that was **then**; this is **now**.

If you can't do what it takes to be successful in Corporate America, then maybe you'd better give serious thought about not taking a job in industry. We want you to be successful, but you must do it in **our** world. You must be able to **convert** in order to be successful. It's not difficult. Once you learn it, you will enjoy it. Think about how much you like hearing people use your first name.

Knowing How To Perform
People are the most important asset a company has. A company wants performers. Companies ask me to bring them individuals with outstanding work ethics. These are people who get out of bed eager to go to work — with strong, positive mental attitudes, and most of all, the ability to **work smart**.

It is critically important, as you make your transition to Corporate America, to demonstrate the ability to be a **peak performer**. Corporations want smart workers, not **workaholics**. They want workers who are well-organized, know how to prioritize, and can effectively manage their time to get their work done in the minimum eight-hour workday.

Don't think for a moment you're not going to work hard. But, as you reach the point where you are competitive with your age group, have gained industry knowledge, and have brought your advanced education level to where it needs to be, then it's time to bring your work and family life into balance. Stress the **quality** of life. Don't burn yourself out on the way to the top. Be **smart**. Perform effectively. Enjoy your new career.

Controlling Your Environment

I watch people come on board as I sit in my favorite seat on Delta or American Airlines and hear them say to themselves, "What seat am I in?" Then, they moan because they are in row 35 or 39. I often think to myself, "They had an opportunity to tell the reservation clerk where they wanted to sit. Why didn't they?"

Applicants tell me, "I had a restless night because my room was next to the coke machine," or "My room was next to the stairway," or "My room was next to the ice machine." I wonder, "Why are you allowing a desk clerk to put you wherever he/she wants to put you?" Control your environment.

CORPORATIONS WANT "TAKE CHARGE" PEOPLE

Applicants give excuses about why they didn't accomplish an objective. It's always someone else's fault. "Someone didn't tell me what to do. Someone didn't get this done." I scratch my head and say, "Why aren't you controlling your own environment?" Sure, there is no ideal system, no perfect world where we can control everything we do. You would be surprised how many things you can control if you make the effort. It will be difficult for you to be successful in Corporate America if you don't learn to control your environment.

I remember one of the great leaders in Corporate America. He never let a problem come to his office except within a designated time of one half-hour in the morning and one half-hour in the afternoon. If the problem didn't surface during those times, he would not handle it until the next half-hour session. He refused to allow problems or situations to control his environment. I have no doubt that's the reason he had the ability to start his career at a large company and go on to become a great leader at one of the best-managed companies in the country. I learned valuable lessons from him.

Too often, I see individuals whose lives have been so controlled by others that they have forgotten how to control their own destiny. So many of you tell me about the difficulty of organizing and controlling your day. I believe it is difficult, but if you intend to be highly successful in Corporate America, you must learn to **control your environment**.

Computer Literacy

Corporate America has begun to **demand** a high degree of computer literacy from all development candidates. Quite simply, because our world is becoming so technologically dependent, the industry **leaders** of the future must be able to function in a complex, rapidly-changing environment. The boom in computer use and technology has touched all of business. You will be handicapped if you are learning **both** your job **and** new technology when you start. Today, applicants with strong computer literacy will have the opportunity to apply for 38 percent more positions than those without it. **Think what it will be like in the near future**.

Due to the changing nature of technology, "literacy" no longer means knowing how to tear apart a mainframe computer. Most people in industry use personal computers (PCs) that are networked with a mainframe they never see or are connected via local area networks (LANs). Therefore, our guidelines focus on ways to improve your literacy through PCs.

Learning On The Most Available PC

The quickest way to learn is to sit down in front of a PC and practice. Don't even consider graduating without taking electives in data processing and having a good aptitude and ability to work with PCs. Because industry is predominantly IBM or IBM compatible, you should practice with hardware and software you will be using in industry. Specifically:

- Become familiar with Disk Operating System (DOS).

- Learn how to work with one of the more popular applications in each of the three major business software categories: word processing, database, and spreadsheet.

In addition to college credit courses, computer courses in continuing education are offered at colleges and universities. Computer classes are also offered by training companies or individuals who specialize in this area. Software manufacturers often produce manuals with tutorials and/or tutorial tapes. You can also find third-party books that give excellent information about the software that interests you. While hands-on practice with DOS and other software is invaluable, you will also benefit from taking courses in basic computer theory, languages, and programming. We recommend some combination of the following: Beginning Computers, PC Skills, and Programming (BASIC, COBOL, or Pascal). It is difficult to be more specific because each case is unique, and course offerings vary significantly from school to school.

Buying A Personal Computer

We strongly recommend that you buy a PC. The following are suggestions to consider in making your purchase:

- Carefully determine where you want to buy. You can't go wrong with one of the national chains if your location puts you close to one of their outlets. If an outlet is not available, there are many excellent smaller dealers. You should really investigate their concept of service. Ask to speak to previous customers. Avoid stores that appear unprofessional — they probably are. Also, there are several excellent mail-order companies with toll-free phone numbers that are **very** competitive on price and quality.

• Buy an IBM or an IBM **compatible**. However, be careful of **cheap** versus **compatible** imitations.

• The following hardware is strongly recommended and is worth the price, though at the time the cost may seem high: 2-4 MB RAM, 20-40 mg hard drive, and letter-quality printer.

• The following software is also suggested: WordPerfect or Microsoft Word for word processing, Lotus 1-2-3 or Excel for spreadsheet, and DBase IV or Paradox for database. Some of the best return on your investment will be in the right software. **Include** its price in your budgeting.

Finally, remember **you** must develop your literacy. No one can do it for you.

Answering Machines

Today, more than ever before, we have to be extremely concerned about time. We are being asked to do more and more work — you, I, and everyone else — in minimum time. Answering machines are indispensable devices that save people a lot of time and frustration trying to reach others. Recruiters spend a tremendous amount of time on the telephone calling applicants. If an applicant is not in and has no answering machine for messages, the recruiter may not call back.

As an example of the problems we encounter when others take messages for applicants, consider the attempts I've made to leave messages with individuals who answer phones at dormitories and sorority or fraternity houses. Often I leave a message, and if I ask the individual to read it back, he or she says, "I'm sorry. I don't have a pencil." This is a situation which is easily solved with an answering machine. You can't ensure that a friend, dorm mate, spouse, or parent will always be available and committed to take messages for you in a professional manner. My recommendation is that you view an answering machine purchase as a must.

A recruiter I know said that when he calls an applicant and there is no answering machine, he will not call back again. He feels the applicant is telling him he really doesn't care about the recruiter's time. He is not willing to use his time or his associate's time making numerous follow-up telephone calls to reach the applicant when there are other applicants with whom he can communicate. He suspects that an applicant today who doesn't have an answering machine probably doesn't believe in computers either.

As you prepare for your job search, consider purchasing an answering machine that has remote capability. If you are traveling on follow-up interviews, you can call in and receive your messages. Once your search is completed, you can dispose of the answering machine, but I doubt that you will. I believe you will be convinced of its convenience.

During a career search, record a message on your answering machine that is very professional. Come to the point so recruiters or their associates can leave a message and go on about their business. It is not appropriate to use flamboyant messages that demonstrate your talents as a comedian or your love of music. While amusing in a social setting, these messages waste a recruiter's valuable time and do not present the business image you need to project. Also, consider setting your answering machine so that it picks up calls after the first ring. There's no need to waste someone's time when you're not there to answer.

> **Your performance characteristics are like staves of a barrel. Your value is worth the shortest stave. — R. Cameron**

Let's Get Motivated

I believe God has given us the right to get out of bed in the morning and be happy or unhappy. It's our choice, but there are a lot of people who must not realize they have this choice. Being in the business of recruiting and evaluating people, I observe people wherever I go — airports, hotels, athletic activities, and meetings. I have been saddened by the people who feel the burden of the world is planted squarely on their shoulders. Whenever I've had that feeling, I have forced myself to lift my head and think about others less fortunate. I would then ask myself, "Do I have the right to feel sorry for myself?" Interestingly enough, 99 times out of 100, the answer was "no." This simple exercise has been very helpful to me in developing an appreciation for life and my work. I love getting out of bed in the morning. I love what I do. I love meeting people. I love the challenges that come to me every day. I like the fact that I can meet challenges head on, look them straight in the eye, and rarely fail. It's fun to be successful, to be alive, to know I can make it happen. If I visualize what I want, I can get it. I feel I am like the majority of the world's population — I have average skills. But, I have performed far above average because of one factor — desire.

I interview many outstanding men and women who have had but a fraction of the success they could have had with their outstanding credentials. People come to me and tell me they should be successful because of their wonderful talents and abilities. I'm very quick to point out they can go to any unemployment line in America and find people with equally as much ability, maybe even more, but, because of the lack of desire to apply those abilities, they are in the unemployment line. I believe that most of them are there because they lack the desire to apply God-given abilities and developed skills. I have an acquaintance who has been very successful and is quite wealthy, yet he was born with a severe handicap. He is an individual who won't accept a physical handicap as an excuse not to be successful. Many of us complain that we don't have everything we want. We look around and see those people who have a lot less than we have from the standpoint of intellect, appearance, or physical features, yet they are more successful than we are. Ever wonder why? Do you have any doubt it is simply a greater **desire** to succeed?

Many people never take responsibility for their own actions. They're the people who, at the end of their lives, look back and feel that life cheated them because they didn't receive everything that was due them. I disagree with this attitude. I feel there is absolutely nothing you can't do if you envision your ability to do it. As I have said in this book before, you must have a make-it-happen personality.

> **Five percent of the people make it happen.**
> **Ten percent of the people watch things happen.**
> **Eighty-five percent don't care what happens.**

Young people often cheat themselves by letting seconds, minutes, days, weeks, and months of their lives go by and not living life to the fullest. They are not reaching out to learn, grow, do, and have. They are choosing to be unhappy versus happy.

At one of my career conferences in Austin, Texas, a new corporate recruiter asked me, "Roger, who pays for the applicants to come to the conference?" I said, "The applicants pay their own way." She asked, "Who pays for their room and board?" I replied, "The applicants pay for their room and board." She said, "Well, why would a young man fly all the way from Colorado Springs to Austin to interview and show absolutely no enthusiasm or excitement? His voice level was so low I had to turn off my air conditioner in order to hear him. He acted as if someone should give him an offer just because he existed. As a matter of fact, I suggested to him that if he thought Corporate America was simply going to hire him because of his credentials, then why was he there? Why didn't he just send a resume? After all, we could see his credentials on a resume. We would just mail him an offer or a decline through the mail." This is a true story, and one that is embarrassing to me. After all, I had recruited him to begin with. Obviously, it was **my** mistake.

It is difficult for me to imagine why anybody would spend $350 to travel across the country and not accomplish the ultimate objective. This young man interviewed with 11 companies, and 11 companies declined him basically for the same reason. He just wasn't enthusiastic. He didn't act as if he was excited to be alive.

If you don't have time in your life to grow or to do the things that make you a better person, you had better examine your life. God only gives us one chance on this earth. If I could motivate just one person who reads this book to reach out and find ways to improve, the book will have been a success. I have absolutely no doubt the book will make people better interviewees, but I want much more than that. I want the book to give you a can-do attitude and to motivate you to choose the best of the two options you have every morning. Remember, when life is over and you look back, if you have not accomplished what you had hoped to, it was because you cheated yourself. Don't let that happen. Every day that goes by is a day you will never be able to live over again.

Tomorrow morning, when you wake up and have the choice to make it a good day or a bad day, make the right decision. I know an individual who, when she leaves her bedroom, crosses an imaginary line on the floor outside her bedroom door. As she crosses that line, she is consciously aware it is her choice to make her day whatever she wants it to be. I have rarely seen her not accomplish her objective. Every day is a positive day. She is motivated. She accomplishes difficult objectives. At the end of the day, she feels good about reaching the goals she has established for herself. Put that imaginary line outside your bedroom door. Be conscious of your choices as you step across it every day.

In conclusion, I strongly recommend you take firm control. Be a catalyst and motivate yourself to accomplish the objectives you want for yourself and your family. Read motivational books. Consider spending some money early in your career on seminars to learn from some of the very best America has to offer. Most of all, when you wake up in the morning, be sure you make the right decision.

Marching Orders

During the course of this book, I have suggested ways to handle certain questions and situations. **Under no circumstance am I suggesting that you use my words.** Every thought or idea should be digested and put into your **own** words, your own manner of delivery. No recruiter wants a person to use someone else's words. There may be certain cases where certain phrases are used, but we encourage applicants to be themselves. You are a unique individual, and you must interview as that unique individual.

I feel you have several selves — you at your best, you at your average, and you at your worst. Interview at your best. To be your best at anything you do, you must be thoroughly prepared. Be committed to what you're doing and focus on your objective.

I encourage you to start early to prepare for any difficult objective. Don't wait until the last minute. Prepare as early as you can in your career for any potential changes you might make. Be conscious, as you go through college, of what you do specifically and uniquely. As you interview, you will present yourself with quality insight. Be aware of the skills you use — organizational ability, prioritizing, effective time management, etc. — and the procedure you apply each time you solve any problem.

Use a tape recorder to verbalize answers before you get in front of corporate recruiters. Never be embarrassed by the fact that you must practice to be concise and articulate. Preparation for anything you do in life only makes you a better person. I've never heard of anyone who gained success in becoming a better student, sorority president, skier, or speaker without practice. I've never known preparation to be embarrassing. All I have ever heard is, "Boy, that person really worked hard to be successful." That's right. That's exactly what it takes.

Come to Corporate America with a high degree of enthusiasm. Have self-confidence and poise in knowing yourself. I encourage you to become consciously aware of who you are. Have accurate self-insight. Be able to communicate in a forceful manner so we will not only hear what you say, but we will believe it as well.

Know what you have done in high school and college and what has made you successful. The better you know yourself and how you have accomplished difficult objectives, the better you can apply that information to any career objectives — in Corporate America, civil service, or your own business.

I hope you've enjoyed this book. I hope you feel better prepared now that you have read it. Best of luck to you.

> **Get in competitive condition
> by thorough preparation.
> Believe in yourself.
> Be positive. Think success.**

Appendix A

DEFINITIONS OF CRITICAL CHARACTERISTICS

Assertiveness: your ability to take charge and present opinions forcefully and persuasively. As previously mentioned, many individuals say the right thing, but not in a believable manner.

Conflict/Resolution: your ability to resolve differences of opinion while maintaining good relationships and attaining goals with peers, superiors, and subordinates alike.

Decision-Making: your thought process (conceptual and analytical) used in solving problems and making decisions. Your ability to make decisions is often brought out in interviews through the use of "Why?" questions.

Decisiveness: your willingness to commit yourself and when asked, make definite choices; your ability to let us know where you stand on issues; not tentative.

Energy/Enthusiasm: your animation, demonstrated by your walk, handshake, and verbal enthusiasm.

Goal Setting/Accomplishments: your ability to establish and accomplish meaningful, attainable goals, overcoming adversity, if necessary.

Initiative: your active efforts to influence events rather than passively accepting them; self-starting, not needing constant prompting from superiors.

Innovativeness/Creativeness: your ability to be a visionary and to keep your eye on the big picture versus having tunnel vision. The desire and ability to move into unchartered waters. Without these two traits, you are a follower instead of a leader.

Intelligence: your conceptual ability, breadth of knowledge, verbal expression, depth of response, analytical thought process.

Maturity: your capacity to exercise emotional control and self-discipline, and your ability to behave realistically. Youth is unfairly and frequently associated with immaturity. You will always have the burden of proof in all interviews.

Openness: your ability to discuss shortcomings as well as strengths, to not be preoccupied with saying the right thing, and to be consistently responsive regardless of content. Recruiters don't want to wonder if there is a hidden meaning to your words. We hire people who "lay the cards" on the table tactfully and professionally.

Oral Communication Skills: your effectiveness of expression; your ability to deliver in a fluid, articulate, succinct, and persuasive manner.

Planning/Organization: your effectiveness in planning and organizing your own activities and those of a group. Your ability to establish an effective, efficient cause of action.

Poise/Self-Confidence: your ease in communicating during the interview. Recruiters want to see that you are comfortable under pressure.

Self-Insight: your ability to accurately perceive, understand, and communicate your strengths and weaknesses.

Sensitivity: your sincerity, friendliness, tactfulness, and responsiveness; your ability to **listen** as well as speak. Be sure in interviews that you are sensitive to recruiters' signals, such as diverting their eyes, shuffling papers, or constantly looking at their watches. They will always give you a signal.

Team Player: your ability to function in a team environment; your demonstrated attitude of ensuring success to those around you equal to your own.

Tough-Mindedness: your ability to make tough, emotionally difficult business and people decisions.

Appendix B

RECOMMENDED READING LIST

Corporate America wants broad-minded, well-read managers. You must develop depth and breadth, and reading is the first step toward achieving greater success.

The books and periodicals listed here are very current in business, and I recommend them to you. However, they are **under no circumstances** the only ones or the specific ones you should read. Following each title are comments which explain why I feel the book or periodical is better than others.

1. **Magazines and Newspapers**

   A. *Fortune.* I recommend *Fortune* over *The Wall Street Journal*, *Business Week*, *Forbes*, and others because it focuses on the trenches of industry, where you'll start, as opposed to corporate finance and merger and acquisition news. The others are excellent but just not as immediately applicable.

   B. *USA Today.* Good for a broad-brush national news review.

   C. A Regional Newspaper. To complement *USA Today*, it helps to understand regional and local news. Shy away from small-town locals and find a metropolitan-based daily (Atlanta, Dallas, Washington, D.C.). Often, these major dailies have a "Week in Review" section on Sunday that provides a great synopsis.

2. **General Business Books**

   A. *In Search of Excellence* (Peters and Waterman). A must read for all. It prescribes eight principles that, while apparently common sense, are in use in only the "best" companies. This book uses personal examples and is very easy to read — even fun. This book has transcended the best-seller list to become a classic.

B. *A Passion for Excellence* (Peters and Austin). This book and *Search* are virtually always mentioned as a two-volume set, but fewer have read *Passion*, and it is, in fact, more useful. It will give you specific ways to implement ideas voiced in *Search*. Pay attention to "Things to do now."

C. *Thriving On Chaos* (Peters). This Tom Peters book addresses ways to adapt to the changing world business climate and is an easy read.

D. *The Renewal Factor* (Waterman). *Renewal* is written to the same issues as *Thriving* but with (again) eight themes divided into sections. This may become a classic.

E. *GMP: The Greatest Management Principle in the World* (LeBoeuf). Once you read it, you'll realize how uncommon it is to see common sense in practice. This book is easy to read, short, and fun.

F. *Dress for Success* and *The Woman's Dress for Success* (John Molloy). You will not make it if you don't dress the part, and I think you may be surprised at how many misconceptions you have. Refer to it as you build your wardrobe. Always remember to err (if you must) on the conservative side.

G. *Reinventing the Corporation* (Naisbitt and Aburdene). This book is very interesting and forward-thinking, and it will help you switch gears and start thinking like your future peers in industry. It also sheds excellent light on the expanding role of women in industry and corporate involvement in quality of life issues.

H. *World Class Manufacturing* (Schonberger). A must read for all manufacturing and operations candidates. This book, and the principles it espouses, are on the lips of virtually all of the forward-thinking corporations. You must understand Total Quality and Just In Time (JIT) concepts. In addition, you may want to read *Japanese Manufacturing Techniques*, also by Schonberger, which includes some excellent examples.

I. *Quality Without Tears* (Crosby). All applicants, especially those considering manufacturing, must appreciate Corporate

America's focus on quality. The real key to profitability is not inspection, but prevention.

J. *Ten Greatest Salespersons* (Shook). This book is **crucial** for **sales** interviewees. Shook interviewed some of the world's greatest sales people (folks from IBM, Xerox, Avon, etc.), and he makes some excellent points. Serving the customer and service after the sale are important concepts to grasp here.

K. *Strategic Selling* (Miller and Herman). Considered the best professional approach to selling in many years, it will virtually give you a master's in selling overnight. Highly recommended by many Fortune 100 companies, this is mandatory reading for applicants considering sales & marketing.

L. *The Other Guy Blinked* (Enrico). This book is a wonderful business story of how Pepsi beat Coca Cola in the cola wars that started a few years ago. It is fun and easy to read. The book is very enlightening to those aspiring to a career in marketing.

M. *The Black Manager* (Dickens and Dickens). An outstanding book for blacks going into Corporate America, for blacks being managed by whites, and whites being managed by blacks. Floyd Dickens speaks from a very successful career with Procter & Gamble. We strongly recommend its valuable insight.

N. *The 7 Habits of Highly Effective People* (Covey). Discover how to free yourself from the weaknesses of others while taking responsibility for your own life.

O. *The Empowered Manager* (Block). Tells how to get employees at all levels to take responsbility for themselves and to show initiative rather than waiting for orders from above.

P. *The Borderless World* (Ohmae). Understand better the changing world economy and Ohmae's hopes for a "borderless world."

Q. *Competitive Advantage* (Porter). A must reading for those fearing their businesses will stop growing.

R. *The Fifth Discipline* (Senge). The fifth discipline — systems thinking — is the cornerstone of the learning organization. Learn how to gain and sustain an advantage by practicing personal mastery, mental models, shared vision, and team learning.

And, finally, three classics that stand by themselves, and that everyone should read, keep, and refer to:

S. *How to Win Friends and Influence People* (Carnegie). Everybody has heard of this one. While many have read it, not all have put it into action. It is outstanding and gives you specific suggestions for improvement.

T. *The Power of Positive Thinking* (Peale). Any high achiever will tell you that you must think positively **first** to get positive results. Visualize success and it will happen.

U. *Top Performance* (Ziglar). Actually, anything by Ziglar is great reading as a motivational book, but this one gives you plenty of tools and tips to beat the competition.

RECOMMENDED SEMINARS AND TAPES

Seminars:

The following are names and addresses of presenters as well as a listing of some of the seminars they offer:

* Topics:
 The Power of Persuasion
 Career
 Time Management
 Presenters: Walter Hailey and Ralph Moten

 Planned Marketing Associates
 P. O. Box 345
 Hunt, Texas 78024
 1-800-749-7621

* Topics:
 The Psychology of Leadership
 Success Secrets of High Achievers
 Presenter: Brian Tracy

 Brian Tracy Learning Systems
 462 Stevens Avenue, Suite 202
 Solana Beach, California 92075-2065

* Topics:
 The Psychology of Winning
 The Winner's Edge
 Winning for Life
 Being the Best
 *The New Dynamics of Winning: Gaining the Mindset of a
 Champion*
 Presenter: Denis Waitley

 Denis Waitley, Inc.
 P. O. Box 197
 Rancho Santa Fe, California 92067
 1-619-756-4201, 1-619-756-5969
 FAX 1-619-756-9717

- Topics:
  See You at the Top
  How to Stay Motivated
  Presenters: Zig Ziglar and Jeff Conley

  Zig Ziglar Corporation
  3330 Earhart Drive, #204
  Carrollton, Texas 75006-5026
  1-214-233-9191
  1-800-527-0306

- Topic: *Increasing Human Effectiveness II*
  Presenter: Bob Moawad

  Edge Learning Institute
  2217 N. 30th Street
  Tacoma, Washington 98403
  1-206-272-3103
  Outside Washington: 1-800-858-1484

The following videos and audiotapes emphasize self-improvement and are available through the Nightingale-Conant Corporation, 7300 North Lehigh Avenue, Chicago, Illinois 60648-9951.

Videotapes:

- *The Magic Word: Attitude* by Earl Nightingale
  Videocassette (43 min.) with two audiocassettes and two guides. Teaches you how to develop and maintain your game plan for success — a good attitude.

- *GOALS: Setting and Achieving Them on Schedule* by Zig Ziglar
  Videocassette (70 min.) helps you receive and set your goals and write your "business plan for life."

- *The Master Key to Success* by Napolean Hill
  Two videocassettes and four audiocassettes with workbook. Provides classic achievement principles that show success is no accident.

Audiotapes:

- *Unlocking Your Potential* by Bob Moaward
  Five audiocassettes for ages 14 and up. Gives teenagers a solid foundation in goal setting and positive thinking.

- *The Psychology of Achievement* by Brian Tracy
  Six tapes plus workbook. Teaches seven basic laws of achievement. Helps you identify your "area of excellence."

- *The Power of Positive Thinking* by Norman Vincent Peale
  Six audiocassettes with listener's guide. An all-time classic to help you increase your confidence in what you can accomplish.

- *Working Smarter* by Michael LeBoeuf
  Six audiocassettes. More than a time management system. Provides specific instructions, simple systems, and valuable psychological tips.

- *The Psychology of Winning* by Denis Waitley
  Six audiocassettes with Progress Guide. Provides ten steps to winning that you can immediately use in every area of your life.

- *The Courage to Live Your Dreams* by Les Brown
  Six audiocassettes. Focuses on how to build good self-esteem by developing a strong vision of yourself and by using positive self-talk.

- *Unlimited Power* by Anthony Robbins
  Six audiocassettes. Contains techniques for breaking self-destructive habits, erasing negative thought patterns, and achieving peak performance.

- *Think and Grow Rich* by Napolean Hill
  Eight audiocassettes, hard-cover book, study guide, and owner's manual. Presents practical, money-making principles used by very successful people.

Appendix C

BEHAVIORAL TRAITS

Use this list to help you determine your behavioral traits.

INTELLIGENT	SERIOUS	RATIONAL
ENERGETIC	INSISTENT	THOUGHTFUL
DECISIVE	CONSCIENTIOUS	POSITIVE
GENIAL	PROFICIENT	SKILLFUL
HARD WORKER	TACTFUL	INTENSE
ASTUTE	WISE	ABSOLUTE
VIGOROUS	ASSERTIVE	INGENIOUS
IMAGINATIVE	CATEGORICAL	FARSIGHTED
SMART	PERCEPTIVE	REASONABLE
GENUINE	COMPETITIVE	DEXTEROUS
CERTAIN	STRONG-WILLED	SOLID
PLUCKY	COMPOSED	DISCERNING
CONVINCING	BRIGHT	PROFOUND
CLEAR	INFLUENTIAL	DECIDED
EFFICIENT	SENSITIVE	INVENTIVE
CLEAR-HEADED	PRODUCTIVE	INDOMITABLE
COMMON SENSE	RESPONSIVE	PRUDENT
EXPLICIT	MAGNETIC	RELENTLESS
SURE	STRONG-MINDED	SENSIBLE
COGNIZANT	DYNAMIC	NOTABLE
DETERMINED	QUICK	SERIOUS
TENACIOUS	VITAL	EXCEPTIONAL
RESOURCEFUL	OPEN	SHARP
CALCULATING	FORCEFUL	SHREWD
KEEN	DOGMATIC	EARNEST
HONEST	TOUGH-MINDED	GRITTY
LIVELY	EMPHATIC	UNFLINCHING
COMPETENT	SINCERE	CONSISTENT

Appendix D

INTERVIEW SELF-EVALUATION

I strongly recommend you evaluate your presentation after each interview to help you immediately determine any deficiencies. Check either "yes" or "no" for each item below. Then, analyze how you can improve for your next interview. **BE HONEST WITH YOURSELF.**

	YES	NO
• Good Impression	___	___
• Good Communication Skills	___	___
• Articulate/Succinct	___	___
• Persuasive	___	___
• Spontaneous	___	___
• Energetic/Enthusiastic	___	___
• Sincere/Genuine	___	___
• Pleasant Personality	___	___
• Positive Attitude	___	___
• Uses First Names	___	___
• Good Listener	___	___
• Honest/High Integrity	___	___
• Illustrates Objective/Subjective Assets	___	___
• Accurate Self-Insight	___	___
• Poised And Self-Confident	___	___
• Creative/Resourceful/Innovative	___	___
• Intelligent/Good Logical Thinker	___	___
• Decisive	___	___
• Long Range Potential (Promotable)	___	___
• Ability To Set Priorities	___	___
• Motivated/Achiever/Drive	___	___
• Not Afraid To Get Hands Dirty - "Hands-On"	___	___
• Organized	___	___
• Analytical Skills/Strategic Thinker	___	___
• Mature/Stable/Good Judgment/Common Sense	___	___
• Ability To Solve Problems	___	___
• Ability To Develop CooperativeRelationships/Team Player	___	___
• Accepts Accountability And Responsibility	___	___
• Leadership/Motivational Skills	___	___
• Perseverance/Good Track Record	___	___
• Accepts Constructive Criticism	___	___
• Keeps Commitments	___	___
• Responsive/Perceptive	___	___
• Make-It-Happen/Goal-Oriented/Results-Oriented	___	___
• Closed Interview	___	___

Appendix E

JOB DESCRIPTIONS

The job descriptions in this appendix are listed under three categories of business occupations according to the U. S. Department of Labor's Standard Occupation Classification: 1) Executive, Administrative, and Managerial Occupations; 2) Engineering, Scientists, and Related Occupations; and 3) Marketing and Sales Occupations. Within each of these classifications are fields of specialty and typical entry-level positions. The following is a brief description of each of the categories and positions.

1. **Executive, Administrative, and Managerial Occupations**

   - *Accounting*—This function controls the financial resources of an organization. Typical entry-level **accounting positions** are:

     - **Junior Auditors**—in public accounting firms, typically review clients' financial statements and provide comments and recommendations about clients' financial systems and control procedures. In private firms, auditors perform operational, financial, and regulation audits.

     - **Junior Tax Accountants**—work in public accounting firms. Prepare tax returns.

     - **Junior Staff Accountants**—work in the accounting department of private organizations. In small firms, work in all accounting areas; in large firms, specialize in one area.

   - *Executive/Administrative Management*—Management's purpose is to accomplish the organization's objectives through developing strategies and directing the efforts of employees.

     - **Management Development Candidates**—complete a management trainee program. If performance is superior, are assigned management positions.

   - *Computer Technology (Data Processing)*—Computer technology is the process of applying computers to solve business and scientific problems. Within an organization, there are three major areas of specialty: operations management, systems analysis, and programming (both systems and application). Typical entry-level **data processing positions** are:

- **Systems Analysts**—design solutions to data processing problems.

- **Programmers**—develop programming for specific internal functions, such as accounts receivable, or programs for sale externally, or plan and design programs to control and maintain a computer system's operating system.

• *Human Resources*—The role of a human resources department is very sophisticated today, including planning and control of employee staffing and the development and utilization of employees. Typical entry-level **human resource positions** are:

- **Job Analysts**—produce job descriptions by first defining the necessary competencies for jobs and then specifying the experience and education levels required.

- **Recruiters**—select employees and place them.

- **Performance Appraisal Specialists**—develop guidelines to follow in conducting performance appraisals.

- **Compensation Analysts**—determine the importance of jobs relative to others and grade and price jobs.

• *Production/Operations* —Production is the process of manufacturing goods from natural resources. Goods can be those used directly by consumers or those used in the manufacture of other products. Manufacturing processes are very complex, requiring specialists in each of three production phases: purchasing, operations, and quality control.

Most production/operations areas in manufacturing companies are organized so that a purchasing department buys the necessary materials for production of their products. The purchasing department is responsible for ensuring the most cost-efficient purchases possible. Typical entry-level **purchasing positions** are:

- **Buyers (or Purchasing Agents)**—report to the purchasing manager and procure materials.

- **Traffic Coordinators**—select the most effective means of transporting goods by analyzing factors such as freight regulations and classifications, schedules, and fees.

Manufacturing facilities are highly automated and complex and require skilled people in the operations area who can determine the most efficient methods of using people, materials, and machines to produce goods. Typical entry-level **operations positions** are:

- **Material Planning Analysts**—schedule the production of goods based on various supply and demand factors with the goal of controlling the amount of capital committed to products inventory.

Global competition for the design and manufacture of quality products is fierce and requires knowledge and skill in analyzing quality control measures and methods and implementing them. Typical entry-level **quality positions** are:

- **Quality Control Managers**—monitor the quality of activities through statistical process control methods to meet specifications and legal requirements. Coordinate with production managers to correct and eliminate product deficiencies.

2. Engineering, Scientists, and Related Occupations

- *Engineering*—Engineering is the process of using scientific principles to create optimal solutions to technical problems. Typical entry-level **engineering positions** are:

    - **Aerospace Engineers**—design, develop, and test aircraft, spacecraft, and missiles.

    - **Chemical Engineers**—design and develop methods of producing chemicals or chemical products and design the factories that produce them.

    - **Civil Engineers**—design and oversee construction of projects, such as bridges, highways, waterworks, sanitary systems, water systems, and tunnels.

- **Electrical Engineers**—design and develop electrical and electronic equipment.

- **Industrial Engineers**—analyze an organization's people, systems, machines, and materials to determine the most efficient way to use these resources.

- **Mechanical Engineers**—design equipment that is power-producing, such as engines, turbines, and motors, and equipment that is power-using, such as air conditioning equipment or machine tools.

- **Nuclear Engineers**—design devices for producing nuclear energy, for processing nuclear fuels, and for disposing of radioactive materials.

3. **Marketing and Sales Occupations**

- *Marketing*—Marketing is the process by which companies manage advertising and public relations activities to present a positive image to the buying public. Typical entry-level **marketing positions** are:

  - **Product/Brand Managers**—develop cost estimates and evaluations of the organization's market and competition for specific products.

  - **Marketing Research Workers**—gather and analyze data about people's spending habits so an organization can make decisions about the design, development, manufacture, and promotion of products or services.

  - **Advertising Specialists**—advertise an organization's products or services.

- *Sales*—Sales is the process of motivating, influencing, and persuading customers to purchase a service or product (either tangible or intangible).

  - **Sales Representatives**—Manufacturers' sales representatives sell a manufacturer's products to other businesses, such as factories or wholesalers or into institutions like schools or hospitals. Wholesale trade salespersons sell products to retailers. For example, a sales representative for an electrical parts wholesaling company may represent several electrical products manufacturers.

A brief description of each of the positions follows.

Accounting Job Descriptions

Junior Auditor

Primary Responsibilities
- Perform typical auditing duties: adding columns of numbers, developing bank reconciliation statements, and counting inventory.
- Count cash.
- Verify receivables.
- In private organizations, perform operational audits requiring observation, surveys, and interviews to investigate job duties and performance.

Qualifications
- Undergraduate degree in accounting or undergraduate degree with a master's in business administration. An undergraduate degree in accounting is acceptable for private accounting.
- Prior experience is an asset.
- Analytical skills.
- Interpersonal skills.
- Ability to work under pressure.
- Computer knowledge and experience.

Junior Tax Accountant

Primary Responsibilities
- Prepare local, state, and individual tax returns and, in some cases, corporate tax returns.
- Master tax law provisions.

Qualifications
- Undergraduate degree in accounting with tax courses, degree in law with a major in tax law, an MBA, or a master's in taxation.
- Prior experience is an asset with auditing experience especially useful.
- Thorough knowledge of the IRS code.
- Knowledge of IRS rulings.
- Analytical skills.

- Interpersonal and communication skills (both oral and written).
- Ability to work under pressure.
- Computer knowledge and experience.

Junior Staff Accountant

<u>Primary Responsibilities</u>
- Prepare financial statements.
- Perform account analysis, journal entries, and bank reconciliations.
- Prepare and file reports with various government agencies.
- Prepare an annual report for the SEC and/or Federal Trade Commission.
- Perform financial analysis functions such as forecasts.

<u>Qualifications</u>
- Undergraduate degree in accounting or master's in business administration.
- Prior experience is an asset.
- Skill in working with numbers.
- Organizational skills.
- Aptitude for working with computers.
- Written and oral communication skills.
- Interpersonal skills.
- Computer knowledge and experience.

Executive/Administrative Management Job Description

Management Development Candidate

<u>Primary Responsibilities</u>
- Develop a detailed understanding of the organization's objectives, systems, people, products, and processes.
- Complete assigned administrative assignments, individual projects, and research projects.

<u>Qualifications</u>
- Undergraduate degree. A master's in business administration may be required.
- Ability to establish visions for the future and identify innovative solutions.
- Ability to work with and direct staff to accomplish tasks.
- Ability to learn rapidly, determine problems and solutions, and identify required training programs for staff.

- Ability to plan and "get the job done."
- Ability to work well and interface effectively with superiors, peers, and subordinates.
- Strong oral and written communication skills.
- Ability to prepare and handle formal presentations.
- Ability to establish priorities, schedules, and methods of control.
- Knowledge and some practical experience with new and emerging technologies.
- Ability to envision practical business application of new technologies.

Computer Technology (Data Processing) Job Descriptions

Systems Analyst

Primary Responsibilities
- Conduct user needs analyses and surveys.
- Analyze hardware and software requirements.
- Recommend technical approaches to meet business needs.
- Provide technical assistance for users.
- Develop user guidelines, standards, and procedures.
- Prepare and present status reports to management.
- Define and prepare specifications.

Qualifications
- Undergraduate degree in computer science.
- Proficiency in one or more relevant programming and control languages.
- Programming or computer systems experience.

Programmer

Primary Responsibilities
- Prepare program design.
- Prepare program code.
- Run program in accordance with test specifications.
- Prepare program documentation.
- Prepare program specifications.
- Enhance/maintain existing programs/systems in accordance with client needs.
- Conduct user needs analysis and surveys.
- Recommend technical approaches to meet business needs.
- Provide day-to-day technical assistance in support of user goals.

- Provide technical training and guidance.
- Prepare and present status reports.

Qualifications
- Undergraduate degree in computer science may be required.
- Demonstrated facility in at least one relevant programming language.
- At least one year of programming experience.

Human Resources Job Descriptions

Job Analyst

Primary Responsibilities
- Develop job descriptions and specifications.
- Use techniques such as Hay's Eight-Point System and the Critical Incident Approach.
- Interview employees.
- Perform computer analysis.

Qualifications
- Undergraduate degree in business administration. An advanced degree in a field, such as business or industrial psychology could be useful.
- Interpersonal and communication skills.
- Computer skills.

Recruiter

Primary Responsibilities
- Interview, test, select, and place employees.
- Promote, transfer, and terminate employees.
- Conduct career counseling regarding relocation.
- Determine job requirements from managers with job openings.
- Determine best recruiting methods.
- Conduct interviews at various college campuses.
- Conduct new employee orientations.

Qualifications
- Undergraduate degree in business administration. An advanced degree in a field such as business or industrial psychology could be useful.

- Excellent interpersonal and communication skills.
- Analytical skills.

Performance Appraisal Specialist

Primary Responsibilities
- Develop guidelines to be followed in performance appraisals.
- Work with people in various departments in the development of performance appraisal systems.
- Work with departments, such as training, to develop workshops to train employees how to use the appraisal system.

Qualifications
- Undergraduate degree in business administration. An advanced degree in a field such as business or industrial psychology could be useful.
- Excellent interpersonal and communication skills.
- Detail orientation and analytical skills.

Compensation Analyst

Primary Responsibilities
- Work with analysts in different departments to analyze jobs.
- Gather information through surveys, observations, and interviews.
- Evaluate the importance of jobs in relation to others and the required skills for them, and write descriptions.
- Grade and price jobs.

Qualifications
- Undergraduate degree in business administration. An advanced degree in a field such as business or industrial psychology could be useful.
- Excellent interpersonal and communication skills.
- Detail orientation and analytical skills.

Production/Operations—Purchasing Job Descriptions

Buyer (or Purchasing Agent)

Primary Responsibilities
- Bid, negotiate, and execute purchases of raw materials, goods, and on-site services for goods.
- Coordinate and collaborate with people involved with engineering applications or capital project management endeavors.

- Select suppliers.
- Maintain inventory of supplies.

Qualifications
- Undergraduate degree in business administration or possibly a technical degree for technically-based companies.
- Previous experience in manufacturing or material management.
- Ability to conduct business with internal and external customers and suppliers consistent with the company's principles and procedures.
- Good communication and persuasive skills.
- Ability and desire to be a team player.
- Knowledge of computerized buying and inventory control systems.
- Mathematics and analytical skills used in analyzing financial cost, writing bids, and calculating cost savings.

Traffic Coordinator

Primary Responsibilities
- Supervise the delivery of goods via established transportation systems, ensuring timeliness.
- Formulate new or improved means of conveyance for transporting products.
- Negotiate favorable service with carriers.

Qualifications
- Undergraduate degree in business may be required.
- Good quantitative skills.
- Computer literacy.

Production/Operations—Operations Job Description

Material Planning Analyst

Primary Responsibilities
- Determine, communicate, and control detailed manufacturing schedules.
- Coordinate with production team to meet dates.
- Analyze material requirements and authorize purchase of materials.
- Ensure timely delivery of parts and minimize inventory.
- Review bill of material for accuracy.
- Publish monthly reports.

Qualifications
- Undergraduate degree.

- Strong communication/negotiation skills.
- Proficiency with PCs.
- Knowledge of just-in-time (JIT) techniques.

Production/Operations—Quality Job Descriptions

Quality Control Manager

Primary Responsibilities
- Assist in specification control of incoming raw materials.
- Monitor raw material flow through the facility and advise plant management in matters involving increasing yield and efficiency.
- Coordinate process control activities with production and maintenance personnel.
- Maintain contact with federal, state, and local regulatory agencies to determine compliance requirements.
- Maintain records and prepare statistical process control reports.
- Initiate and maintain contact with customers who have filed complaints or claims involving poor product quality.
- Coordinate with production managers to correct and eliminate product quality deficiencies.

Qualifications
- Undergraduate degree in business or engineering, depending on the technical nature of the company and product.
- Sound working knowledge in the operation and use of computers and computer technology.
- Skill in managing through communication and cooperation.
- Ability to troubleshoot problems and recommend remedies to quality/production problems.
- Understanding of and ability to communicate statistical quality control methods and concepts.
- Understanding of how production, efficiency, spending, and quality affect profitability.
- Experience in the company's particular industry.

Engineering Job Descriptions

The following generic responsibilities could apply to any engineering position:
- Propose, design, and develop products and/or processes in particular area of expertise, utilizing and applying engineering principles, research data, and proposed specifications. Consider

criteria such as unit performance, cost, weight, ease of manufacture, ease of operation, and maintenance.
- Direct preparation of required drawings, schematics, and specifications.
- Make design calculations and/or calculations required by certification organization.
- Write specifications for materials and purchased items.
- Direct and coordinate manufacture of assigned project. Act as liaison and technical advisor to various departments throughout the production process.
- Ensure that time schedules are met.
- Plan and develop test procedures.
- Analyze test data to determine if design meets functional and performance specifications, and report results.
- Prepare design modifications on existing components as required.
- Ensure quality control on assigned projects, including making determinations on salvageability of out-of-tolerance components.
- Specify level of acceptable quality. Resolve operational problems of the products designed.
- Prepare operating and maintenance manuals for assigned projects.
- Develop a basic knowledge of field operations and manufacturing processes with area of expertise.
- Travel to international and domestic locations to provide technical assistance and/or training to field personnel or customers.
- Provide training in operation of new equipment. May prepare curriculum and present classroom instruction on various technical topics.
- Prepare a variety of reports, including monthly time report, weekly status report, and engineering bulletins.
- Utilize computer applications to solve certain engineering problems.
- Analyze data to determine feasibility of product proposal, considering specifications, cost, and time constraints.
- Conduct research and testing to clarify or resolve problems and develop design.

Aerospace Engineer

Primary Responsibilities
Responsibilities may include the following:
- Design, develop, and test aircraft, spacecraft, and/or missiles.
- Coordinate projects with scientists, such as physicists or metallurgists, and with engineers in other fields.
- Supervise technicians and drafters.

Qualifications

- Undergraduate degree in aerospace, aeronautical, or astronautical engineering. Some positions require an advanced degree.
- State licensing is required for engineers whose work affects the life, health, or property of others. To receive the license, an engineer must have a degree from an accredited school, complete four years of engineering experience, and pass a state examination.
- Some companies require a security clearance.

Chemical Engineer

Primary Responsibilities

- Design and develop methods of producing chemicals or chemical products.
- Design and supervise the construction of factories that produce chemicals and chemical products.
- Estimate power and labor requirements to operate plants.
- Conduct scientific experiments to calculate atmospheric conditions such as temperature.
- Consult with chemists.
- Analyze the environmental effects of a plant's processes.
- Design and build pilot plants to test equipment and experiment with new methods.
- Develop solutions to production problems.
- Develop and monitor quality standards.

Qualifications

- Undergraduate degree in chemical engineering. Some positions require an advanced degree. A master's in business administration may be helpful if a management position is desired.
- State licensing is required for engineers whose work affects the life, health, or property of others. To receive the license, an engineer must have a degree from an accredited school, complete four years of engineering experience, and pass a state examination.

Civil Engineer

Primary Responsibilities

- Design and oversee construction of projects such as bridges, highways, waterworks, sanitary systems, water systems, and tunnels.
- Apply standard civil engineering practices and techniques, adjust and correlate data, recognize discrepancies and results, and follow operations through a series of related, detailed steps or processes.

<u>Qualifications</u>
- Undergraduate degree in civil engineering.
- State licensing is required for engineers whose work affects the life, health, or property of others. To receive the license, an engineer must have a degree from an accredited school, complete four years of engineering experience, and pass a state examination.

Electrical Engineer

<u>Primary Responsibilities</u>
- Design and develop electrical and electronic equipment.
- Test equipment.
- Supervise the production of equipment.
- Develop schedules and performance requirements.
- Oversee the building of power generation plants and installation of equipment
- Supervise manufacturing of equipment.

<u>Qualifications</u>
- Undergraduate degree in electrical or electronics engineering. Some positions require an advanced degree. A master's in business administration may be helpful if a management position is desired.
- State licensing is required for engineers whose work affects the life, health, or property of others. To receive the license, an engineer must have a degree from an accredited school, complete four years of engineering experience, and pass a state examination.

Industrial Engineer

<u>Primary Responsibilities</u>
- Analyze an organization's people, systems, machines, and materials to determine the most efficient way to use these resources.
- Develop solutions to technical manufacturing and human relationship problems.
- Consult with other departments in the organization (such as production, engineering, and management) to gather information about operations.
- Study operating requirements (cost, timing, quality, etc.).
- Design data processing systems.
- Develop systems that aid in financial planning and cost analysis.
- Develop production planning and control systems and physical distribution systems.

- Develop job appraisal systems and wage and salary administration systems.
- Analyze factors influencing location of plants.

Qualifications
- Undergraduate degree in industrial engineering or another engineering field. An advanced degree in engineering or business administration is desirable. Some positions require a doctorate.
- Good communication skills.
- Good problem-solving skills.
- Must be able to synthesize details to formulate a "big picture" view.
- State licensing is required for engineers whose work affects the life, health, or property of others. To receive the license, an engineer must have a degree from an accredited school, complete four years of engineering experience, and pass a state examination.

Mechanical Engineer

Primary Responsibilities
- Design equipment that is power-producing, such as engines, turbines, and motors.
- Design equipment that is power-using, such as air conditioning equipment or machine tools.
- Design equipment used in transmitting power.
- Coordinate projects with scientists and technicians.
- Oversee the production, installation, maintenance, operation, and/or sales of equipment.

Qualifications
- Undergraduate degree in electrical or electronics engineering. Some positions require an advanced degree in business administration or a specialized field of engineering.
- State licensing is required for engineers whose work affects the life, health, or property of others. To receive the license, an engineer must have a degree from an accredited school, complete four years of engineering experience, and pass a state examination.

Nuclear Engineer

Primary Responsibilities
- Design devices for producing nuclear energy, for processing nuclear fuels, and/or for disposing of radioactive materials.

- Design and oversee construction of nuclear facilities.
- Work with scientists to develop equipment and processes for nuclear research.
- Solve problems related to nuclear energy.
- Supervise nuclear facility operation.
- Supervise others in the manufacture of nuclear products.

Qualifications
- Undergraduate degree in electrical or electronics engineering. Some positions require an advanced degree in business administration or a specialized field of engineering.
- State licensing is required for engineers whose work affects the life, health, or property of others. To receive the license, an engineer must have a degree from an accredited school, complete four years of engineering experience, and pass a state examination.

Marketing and Sales Job Descriptions

Product Manager

Primary Responsibilities
- Develop promotion plans and a promotion budget.
- Coordinate with plants to determine production needs and develop sales materials for promotions or new products.
- Estimate costs for new products.
- Evaluate market and competition for a specific product.

Qualifications
- Master's in business administration or management.
- Strong background in marketing.
- Interpersonal skills.
- Analytical, strategic, creative, and practical thinking skills.
- Oral and written communication skills.
- Leadership skills.

Marketing Research Worker

Primary Responsibilities
- Conduct field studies and develop questionnaires to determine the reactions, opinions, and suggestions of potential customers about new products or features.
- Analyze the results and report to management.
- Evaluate effectiveness of an organization's marketing methods.

<u>Qualifications</u>
- Undergraduate degree. Courses in economics, statistics, sociology, marketing, and psychology helpful. Advanced degree desirable. For example, B. A. in sociology and M.A. in business administration.
- Interpersonal skills.
- Analytical skills.
- Oral and written communication skills.

Advertising Specialist

<u>Primary Responsibilities</u>
- Create and place ads or act as the liaison between the company and an advertising agency.
- Coordinate with the advertising director for design and development of advertising campaigns.
- Develop goals and budgets for a campaign. May work with an agency to implement the campaign or coordinate with internal staff.
- Conduct market research.
- Track advertising results.
- Communicate advertising publicity to sales department.

<u>Qualifications</u>
- Undergraduate degree in liberal arts or business with courses in marketing, business administration, and communications helpful.

Sales Representative

<u>Primary Responsibilities</u>
- Continually develop strong interpersonal skills and product and territory knowledge.
- Inform management on a regular basis of all sales activities.
- Be familiar with the organization's capabilities to produce products.
- Qualify and prioritize prospects.
- Make sales presentations.
- Prepare proposals.
- Attain annual sales quota.

<u>Qualifications</u>
- Undergraduate degree. Wholesale salespersons may be required by firms such as drug wholesalers to have a technical degree in chemistry, biology, or pharmacy.
- Good sales and communication skills.

- Depending on the nature of the company's business, specific technical knowledge and skill may be required.
- Willingness to travel is often required.
- Physical stamina may be required.
- Math and computer skills are an asset.

Appendix F

SAMPLE RESUME FORMAT

John/Jane Q. Student
Street Address
City, State Zip Code
(Area Code) Home Phone Number

AVAILABLE:
Age:____ ; Height____ ' ____ "; Weight ____ lbs.
Marital Status: _____

(Note: For "Age," put the age you will be at the time you will be interviewing, not your age now.)

EDUCATION
BS/BA (Major)__ (Year Complete)__
University
City, State

MS/MA (Emphasis)__ (Year Complete)__
University
City, State

(Indicate **all** college work — if incomplete degree, state amount completed.)

ACTIVITIES

High School: List the following: all scholastic honors, scholarships, honorary societies (offices held), student body government (offices held), class organizations and clubs (offices held), athletic activities (including awards and honors attained).

College: Include the same information as listed in high school, as well as intramural sports, publications, and assistantships. Also include any community, civic, or church activities as well as the number of hours worked in part-time work while you were in high school and/or college. It is **very important** to submit as much information in the ACTIVITIES section as possible. This information can weigh just as heavily as actual work experience.

Note: ____ % of education financed by scholarship, ____ % by part-time work, ____ % by loan.
(Complete for undergraduate **and** graduate education.)

EXPERIENCE

6/91-9/91: Cashier - Listing the most recent position first, provide date and title of position held. Then, using **10-15 typed lines**, give information about the **specific** responsibilities and supervisory duties (number and type of people supervised), and the amount and **specific** type of equipment used and/or responsible for. Then, list **significant accomplishments** while in each position. Accomplishments can be work and/or personal goals attained or exceeded. Describe each accomplishment in bullet format. Include collateral duties but only as a minority portion of your bullets. Provide at least 2-4 bullets per job.

Sample bullets:
* Graduated as valedictorian of high school class with a 97.9 GPA.
* Achieved "Outstanding Employee of the Year" award.
* Achieved a 3.7 GPA in college.
* Achieved 10% and 12% over goal for fraternity's annual charity fund-raisers in 1990 and 1991, respectively.

Index